ISBN 0·85079·219·3

The Faldo Formula
FROM TEE TO GREEN
with NICK FALDO

150 GOLF LESSONS

from the
Daily Express

£2.95

*T*wo years ago the Daily Express was offered a choice of instructional strips and guests writers...Nick Faldo or Seve Ballesteros. It was no easy decision.

Ballesteros was the prince of charisma, the sweet-swinging Spaniard who seemed destined to dominate the next decade. Faldo by contrast was perceived as the slightly aloof perfectionist, a man still in search of his destiny.

We chose Faldo, partly by instinct, but mainly in optimism because he was British.

How he has repaid that faith!

The Open championship, followed by two US Masters to mark himself as the leading golfer of the Nineties.

Now Faldo shares his secrets with you...the formula which transformed him from fine player to world beater. No matter what your handicap this unique book is guaranteed to help.

David Emery, Daily Express Sports Editor.

*M*any people were bewildered when I decided to restructure my swing completely in the summer of 1985. Two years previously I had won five tournaments and topped the European Order of Merit. Why change?

The old swing had made me one of the best players in Europe, but I had grown increasingly more unhappy with it and particularly when I needed to rely on it the most – in the last nine holes of major championships. I was looking for a swing to win me Grand Slam titles and I was convinced the one I had would not accomplish that.

It was about that time that I began to learn about the teachings of David Leadbetter and I decided to satisfy my curiosity. I introduced myself to him and during that first, brief meeting, David, an Englishman based in Florida, gave me a few thoughts to try.

I was not expecting miracles and after getting nowhere in particular for six months, I made the decision that was to transform my entire career. I asked

David to completely overhaul my swing. In his eyes, and I have never known anybody better at spotting minute details, there was more wrong than right. I knew it was going to take a long time, but two years was longer than even I had anticipated.

There were times in that period when the frustration level was almost unbearable. I was putting in all the long, hard hours on the practice range...and getting nothing for it. The thing that pulled me through as much as anything was my belief in David.

As soon as I could see the slightest improvement, my confidence started to return and grow. There was a light at the end of the tunnel and it was getting brighter. When I emerged from those hard, long months of doubt and frustration, I knew I was in a position to fulfil all the demands I had made of myself as a youngster when I had stood over 10 foot putts and said to myself: "This one for the Open".

It is also why when I did win my first major,

The Open at Muirfield, in 1987, I dedicated it to him. Without his help I could not have done it.

I still practice religiously and see David as regularly as possible, but the long hours working on the basics of the swing are now behind me. When I go to the practice ground now it is to fine tune rather than to work on fundamental details.

Since my win at Muirfield and during my two triumphs in the US Masters at Augusta, it has been my pleasure since then to pass on tips and other things I have learned from David or throughout my career to Daily Express readers through my Faldo Formula series.

I have tried to keep the lessons simple and easy to digest, because there is nothing worse than too much theory buzzing about in a player's mind at one time. If you can practice the things I deal with then, with time, they ought to become second nature.

There is nothing better than seeing a good end result from something that was far from perfect before and if I have helped cut a couple of shots from your handicap after you have read this compilation of my Daily Express series then that will please me.

From scratch to 28, there should be something for everybody in this easy to follow guide to better golf.

The game has given me immense pleasure over the years and hopefully will continue to do so. If I can spread a little happiness and give you a little help along the way then so much the better.

Contents

Edited by Martin Hardy, Daily Express Golf Correspondent

Early Lessons

GOLF IS A GAME IN WHICH CERTAIN FUNDAMENTALS HAVE TO BE OBSERVED IF ANYONE IS TO BECOME A GOOD PLAYER.....

...THE BEST WAY TO LEARN THESE, ESPECIALLY FOR YOUNGSTERS, IS TO INVEST IN A FEW LESSONS FROM YOUR LOCAL PROFESSIONAL....

...HAVING A SOLID GRIP, SET-UP AND SWING RIGHT FROM THE START WILL PAY DIVIDENDS IN THE LONG-RUN.

The Right Equipment

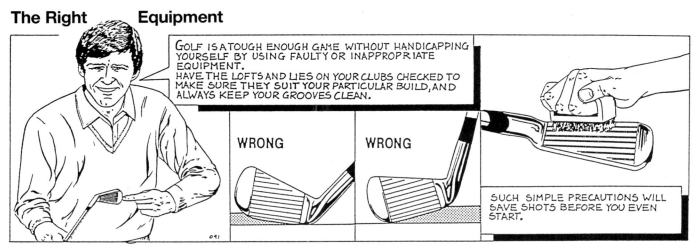

GOLF IS A TOUGH ENOUGH GAME WITHOUT HANDICAPPING YOURSELF BY USING FAULTY OR INAPPROPRIATE EQUIPMENT.
HAVE THE LOFTS AND LIES ON YOUR CLUBS CHECKED TO MAKE SURE THEY SUIT YOUR PARTICULAR BUILD, AND ALWAYS KEEP YOUR GROOVES CLEAN.

WRONG

WRONG

SUCH SIMPLE PRECAUTIONS WILL SAVE SHOTS BEFORE YOU EVEN START.

Bend your Knees

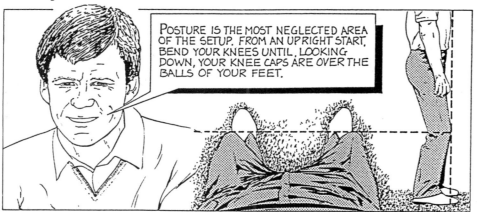

POSTURE IS THE MOST NEGLECTED AREA OF THE SETUP. FROM AN UPRIGHT START, BEND YOUR KNEES UNTIL, LOOKING DOWN, YOUR KNEE CAPS ARE OVER THE BALLS OF YOUR FEET.

THEN BEND FROM YOUR WAIST KEEPING THE SMALL OF YOUR BACK STRAIGHT. THAT IS A GOOD POSITION FROM WHICH TO START A SWING.

Develop a Routine

HAVING A REGULAR ROUTINE BEFORE EACH SHOT IS EXTREMELY IMPORTANT IF ONLY FOR YOUR PEACE OF MIND......

...MY OWN GOES LIKE THIS: ASSESS THE SHOT FROM BEHIND THE BALL, LINE UP THE CLUB SQUARE TO THE TARGET, PLACE BODY PARALLEL TO THE TARGET LINE.....

TARGET LINE

90°

...FIND A SEQUENCE TO SUIT YOUR GAME AND DO IT EVERY TIME.

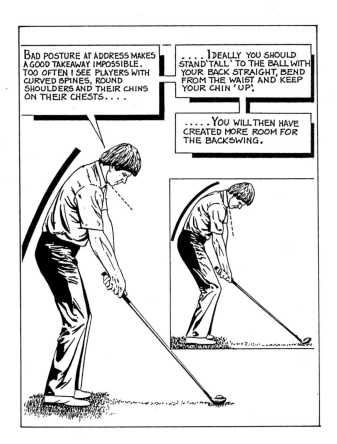

BAD POSTURE AT ADDRESS MAKES A GOOD TAKEAWAY IMPOSSIBLE. TOO OFTEN I SEE PLAYERS WITH CURVED SPINES, ROUND SHOULDERS AND THEIR CHINS ON THEIR CHESTS....

.... IDEALLY YOU SHOULD STAND 'TALL' TO THE BALL WITH YOUR BACK STRAIGHT, BEND FROM THE WAIST AND KEEP YOUR CHIN 'UP'.

..... YOU WILL THEN HAVE CREATED MORE ROOM FOR THE BACKSWING.

A GOOD WAY TO CHECK YOUR POSTURE AT ADDRESS IS TO MAKE SURE YOUR SHOULDERS ARE ABOVE YOUR KNEES.

GET A FRIEND TO PLACE A CLUB AGAINST YOUR RIGHT SHOULDER. IF YOU ARE SET UP CORRECTLY IT SHOULD HIT YOUR RIGHT KNEE.

Posture

Shoulders above Knees

Tee High or Low?

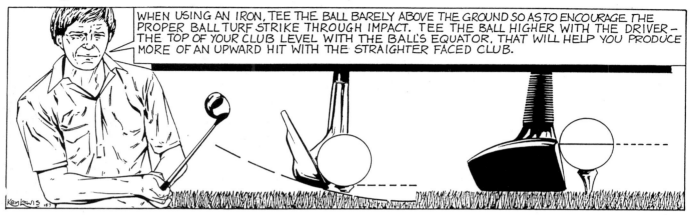

WHEN USING AN IRON, TEE THE BALL BARELY ABOVE THE GROUND SO AS TO ENCOURAGE THE PROPER BALL TURF STRIKE THROUGH IMPACT. TEE THE BALL HIGHER WITH THE DRIVER — THE TOP OF YOUR CLUB LEVEL WITH THE BALL'S EQUATOR. THAT WILL HELP YOU PRODUCE MORE OF AN UPWARD HIT WITH THE STRAIGHTER FACED CLUB.

Poor Alignment

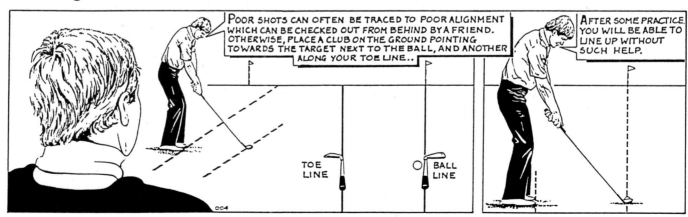

POOR SHOTS CAN OFTEN BE TRACED TO POOR ALIGNMENT WHICH CAN BE CHECKED OUT FROM BEHIND BY A FRIEND. OTHERWISE, PLACE A CLUB ON THE GROUND POINTING TOWARDS THE TARGET NEXT TO THE BALL, AND ANOTHER ALONG YOUR TOE LINE..

TOE LINE

BALL LINE

AFTER SOME PRACTICE, YOU WILL BE ABLE TO LINE UP WITHOUT SUCH HELP.

Swinging all the way through

OBVIOUSLY IT IS DIFFICULT TO HIT GOOD SHOTS IF YOUR INITIAL AIM IS POOR. TO ALIGN YOURSELF SQUARE TO THE TARGET, PICK A POINT A FEW FEET AHEAD OF THE BALL ON YOUR CHOSEN LINE AND AIM AT THAT RATHER THAN THE DISTANT FLAG.

JACK NICKLAUS ALWAYS DOES THIS AND I CANNOT THINK OF A BETTER RECOMMENDATION.

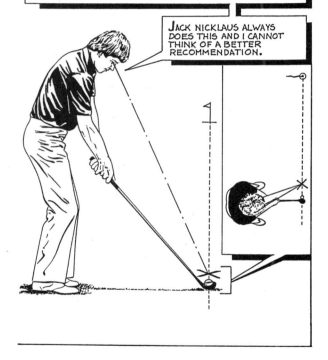

STAYING LOOSE BY WAGGLING THE CLUB SHOULD BE PART OF YOUR PRE-SHOT ROUTINE. IT IS EXTREMELY DIFFICULT TO BEGIN YOUR SWING SMOOTHLY FROM A STATIC POSITION .....

SNATCH

MY OWN WAGGLE IS A REHEARSAL OF MY TAKEAWAY, BUT WHAT YOU DO IS LESS IMPORTANT THAN ACTUALLY DOING SOMETHING. FIND OUT WHAT SUITS YOU BEST AND DO IT "EVERYTIME"

Line up Straight

Waggle the Club

The Address

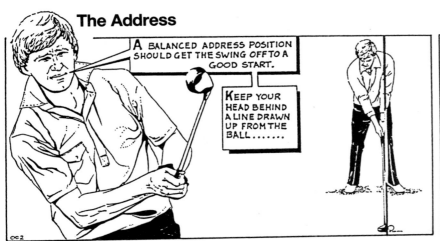

A BALANCED ADDRESS POSITION SHOULD GET THE SWING OFF TO A GOOD START.

KEEP YOUR HEAD BEHIND A LINE DRAWN UP FROM THE BALL......

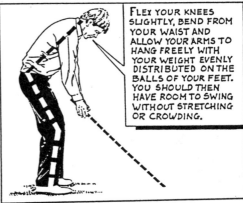

FLEX YOUR KNEES SLIGHTLY, BEND FROM YOUR WAIST AND ALLOW YOUR ARMS TO HANG FREELY WITH YOUR WEIGHT EVENLY DISTRIBUTED ON THE BALLS OF YOUR FEET. YOU SHOULD THEN HAVE ROOM TO SWING WITHOUT STRETCHING OR CROWDING.

The Ball Position

IT IS CLEARLY IMPORTANT TO POSITION THE BALL WITHIN THE STANCE AT THE POINT WHERE THE CLUBFACE WILL BE TRAVELLING SQUARE TO THE TARGET LINE......

THE MORE LOFTED THE CLUB, THE FURTHER BACK TOWARDS THE RIGHT FOOT THE BALL SHOULD BE. THIS IS BECAUSE THE NINE IRON WITH THE SHORTER SHAFT IS SWUNG ON A STEEPER ARC THAN SAY A THREE IRON.

NINE IRON BALL POSITION AND ARC.

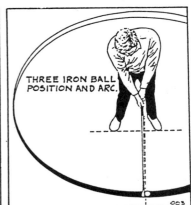

THREE IRON BALL POSITION AND ARC.

Understanding Impact

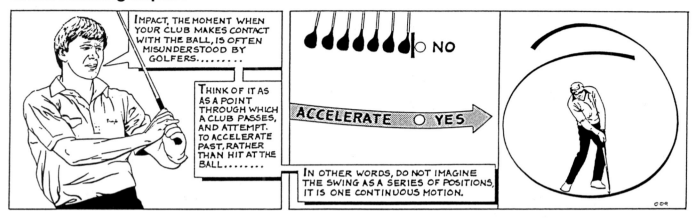

IMPACT, THE MOMENT WHEN YOUR CLUB MAKES CONTACT WITH THE BALL, IS OFTEN MISUNDERSTOOD BY GOLFERS.........

THINK OF IT AS A POINT THROUGH WHICH A CLUB PASSES, AND ATTEMPT TO ACCELERATE PAST, RATHER THAN HIT AT THE BALL........

NO

ACCELERATE ○ YES

IN OTHER WORDS, DO NOT IMAGINE THE SWING AS A SERIES OF POSITIONS, IT IS ONE CONTINUOUS MOTION.

The Grip

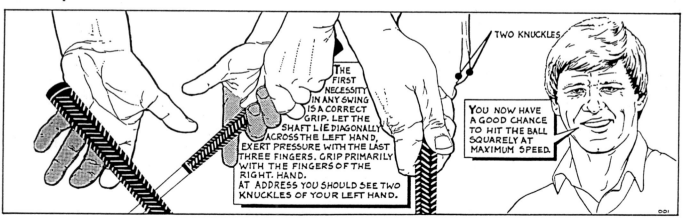

THE FIRST NECESSITY IN ANY SWING IS A CORRECT GRIP. LET THE SHAFT LIE DIAGONALLY ACROSS THE LEFT HAND, EXERT PRESSURE WITH THE LAST THREE FINGERS. GRIP PRIMARILY WITH THE FINGERS OF THE RIGHT HAND.
AT ADDRESS YOU SHOULD SEE TWO KNUCKLES OF YOUR LEFT HAND.

TWO KNUCKLES

YOU NOW HAVE A GOOD CHANCE TO HIT THE BALL SQUARELY AT MAXIMUM SPEED.

e Palms Facing

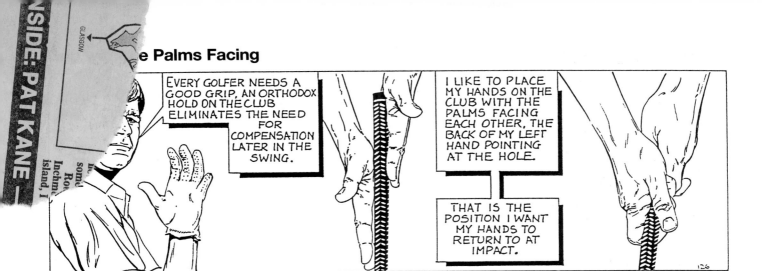

Grip Pressure

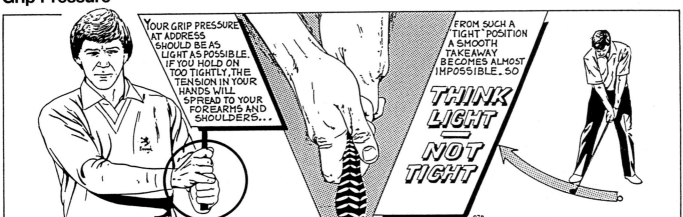

Cut out Tension

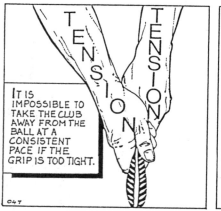

IT IS IMPOSSIBLE TO TAKE THE *CLUB* AWAY FROM THE BALL AT A CONSISTENT PACE IF THE GRIP IS TOO TIGHT.

047

JERKY

..UNNECESSARY PRESSURE TRANSMITS TENSION FROM THE HANDS TO FOREARMS AND USUALLY LEADS TO A JERKY TAKEAWAY..

EXPER... HOW L... GRIP WHILE STILL MAINTAINING YOUR HOLD ON THE CLUB FROM ADDRESS TO TOP OF THE BACKSWING..

Figure of Eight Test

HOW TIGHTLY SHOULD YOU HOLD YOUR CLUB? THE ANSWER IS SIMPLE

I HOLD ON JUST ENOUGH SO THAT NO TENSION CREEPS FROM MY HANDS INTO MY WRISTS.

127.

HOLD A CLUB UP IN FRONT OF YOU AND MAKE A FIGURE OF EIGHT. IF YOU CAN DO THAT SMOOTHLY, YOUR WRIST AND HANDS ARE NICELY RELAXED, READY TO BEGIN THE SWING.

Practice makes perfect

Practice with a Purpose

WHEN YOU ARE PRACTISING, BE CONSTRUCTIVE, PUT A CLUB ON THE GROUND TO AID YOUR ALIGNMENT. HIT BALLS TO A TARGET......

...HIT EVERY SHOT AT THE SAME PACE, WORK THROUGH THE SAME PRE-SHOT ROUTINE EVERY TIME.

IN OTHER WORDS, MAKE HITTING GOOD SHOTS A HABIT NOT AN ACCIDENT.

That Elusive Alignment

HAVING TROUBLE ON THE COURSE? OK THEN BEFORE YOU "FIDDLE" WITH YOUR SWING, CHECK YOU ARE AIMING PROPERLY......

FAULTY ALIGNMENT IS NEARLY ALWAYS THE PRIMARY CAUSE OF POOR SHOTS AND A CLUB PLACED ALONG YOUR TOE-LINE AS YOU SET-UP FOR A PRACTICE SWING CAN OFTEN REVEAL THE ROOT OF THE PROBLEM.

CORRECT

INCORRECT

Challenge Yourself

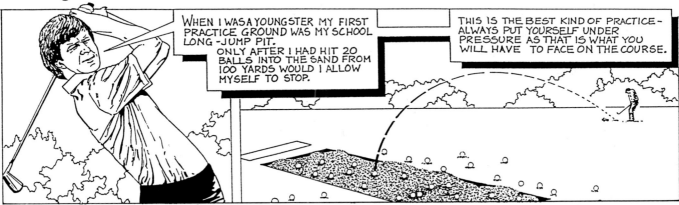

WHEN I WAS A YOUNGSTER MY FIRST PRACTICE GROUND WAS MY SCHOOL LONG-JUMP PIT.
ONLY AFTER I HAD HIT 20 BALLS INTO THE SAND FROM 100 YARDS WOULD I ALLOW MYSELF TO STOP.

THIS IS THE BEST KIND OF PRACTICE - ALWAYS PUT YOURSELF UNDER PRESSURE AS THAT IS WHAT YOU WILL HAVE TO FACE ON THE COURSE.

Wind on the Range

ONLY VERY RARELY IS PRACTISE IN A LEFT TO RIGHT WIND A GOOD IDEA.

BECAUSE THE WIND IS BLOWING OVER YOUR SHOULDER IT WILL EVENTUALLY AFFECT YOUR ALIGNMENT AND CONFIDENCE AS YOU STRUGGLE TO KEEP THE BALL STRAIGHT. SO, IF YOU HAVE A CHOICE, WARM-UP IN A RIGHT-TO-LEFT WIND.

Turn Shoulders after Lay Off

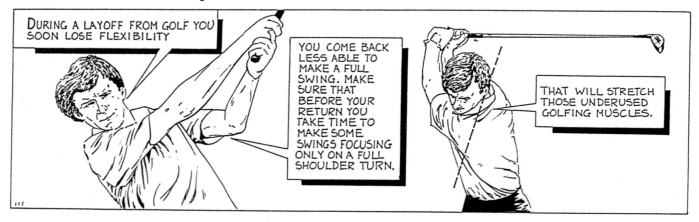

DURING A LAYOFF FROM GOLF YOU SOON LOSE FLEXIBILITY

YOU COME BACK LESS ABLE TO MAKE A FULL SWING. MAKE SURE THAT BEFORE YOUR RETURN YOU TAKE TIME TO MAKE SOME SWINGS FOCUSING ONLY ON A FULL SHOULDER TURN.

THAT WILL STRETCH THOSE UNDERUSED GOLFING MUSCLES.

Play One Ball Against Another

COMPETITIVE PRACTICE IS ALWAYS BETTER THAN SIMPLY STANDING ON THE RANGE BEATING BALLS INTO OBLIVION. IF THE COURSE IS QUIET, HIT TWO BALLS, PLAYING ONE AGAINST THE OTHER. THAT WILL INTRODUCE SOME TENSION INTO WHAT WOULD OTHERWISE BE A ROUTINE GAME.

HOLE	YARDS	BALL	
		A	B
1	346	4	4
2	472	4	5
3	503	6	4
4	153		

Make One Big Divot

WHEN PRACTISING MAKE LIFE EASIER FOR THE GREENKEEPER BY PLAYING ALL YOUR SHOTS FROM VIRTUALLY THE SAME SPOT.

IN THAT WAY YOU'LL MAKE ONE LARGE DIVOT MARK INSTEAD OF LOTS OF SMALLER ONES. IT IS A FAR SIMPLER TASK TO REPLACE ONE LARGE AREA OF TURF RATHER THAN MANY SMALL ONES SPREAD OUT ALL OVER THE PLACE.

Practice without the Ball

SOMETIMES A PLAYERS GRACEFUL PRACTICE SWING BEARS NO RESEMBLANCE TO THE ACTION HE EMPLOYS ON THE ACTUAL SHOT

THE SIGHT OF THE BALL HAS CAUSED TENSION TO CREEP INTO HIS.. ...HANDS.... ARMS.......... SHOULDERS AND LEGS.

PRACTISING MORE WITHOUT A BALL WILL CURE THIS, AND WILL INGRAIN THAT ELUSIVE RHYTHMIC MOTION.

EVENTUALLY YOUR PRACTICE AND 'REAL' SWINGS WILL LOOK THE SAME.

30 Minutes before Tee-Off

Be Specific

Feet Together

IF YOU ARE SWAYING OFF THE BALL SPEND SOME TIME ON THE PRACTICE GROUND HITTING SHOTS WITH YOUR FEET TOGETHER. THIS WILL ELIMINATE YOUR SWAY AS ANY LATERAL MOVEMENT ON THE BACKSWING WILL CAUSE YOU TO FALL OVER........

....ONLY WHEN MAKING A SOLID CONTACT WITH EVERY SHOT SHOULD YOU RETURN TO YOUR NORMAL STANCE.

Warm up on the Tee

IDEALLY EVERY GOLFER SHOULD WARM UP ON THE PRACTICE GROUND BEFORE EACH ROUND. BUT IF YOU DON'T HAVE TIME, HOLD TWO CLUBS TOGETHER AND SWING THEM TO AND FRO ON THE FIRST TEE. THAT SHOULD LOOSEN UP YOUR MUSCLES....

....THEN TAKE A FEW MORE SWINGS WITH A WEDGE CONCENTRATING ON ACCELERATING THROUGH IMPACT.

ACCELERATE

WHEN BAD WEATHER FORCES YOU INDOORS, CONSTRUCTIVE PRACTICE IS STILL POSSIBLE. IN FRONT OF A MIRROR YOU CAN CHECK MANY THINGS: YOUR GENERAL SET-UP, POSTURE, ALIGNMENT, AND BALL POSITION TO NAME BUT A FEW......

DO THIS REGULARLY FOR REASSURANCE AND YOU'LL BE THAT BIT MORE CONFIDENT BACK ON THE COURSE.

EVERYONE CAN LEARN A LOT SIMPLY BY WATCHING THE SWING OF TOP PROFESSIONALS. WHEN YOUNGER I NEVER HESITATED TO COPY SOMETHING I THOUGHT COULD HELP MY GAME.....

.... HOWEVER, ENSURE THAT YOU COPY A SIMILAR SWING PLANE TO YOUR OWN. IF YOU ARE FAIRLY TALL STUDY SOMEONE LIKE GREG NORMAN, SHORTER PEOPLE CAN LEARN FROM, SAY, IAN WOOSNAM.

In a Mirror

Watch and Learn

Transferring my weight to the left side – that's right

Shut that Door

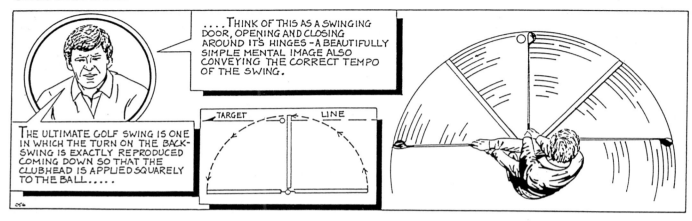

.... THINK OF THIS AS A SWINGING DOOR, OPENING AND CLOSING AROUND IT'S HINGES - A BEAUTIFULLY SIMPLE MENTAL IMAGE ALSO CONVEYING THE CORRECT TEMPO OF THE SWING.

THE ULTIMATE GOLF SWING IS ONE IN WHICH THE TURN ON THE BACK-SWING IS EXACTLY REPRODUCED COMING DOWN SO THAT THE CLUBHEAD IS APPLIED SQUARELY TO THE BALL.....

TARGET LINE

Swing-Path with Divot Check

IF YOUR SHOTS ARE INCONSISTENT THEN THE PROBLEM MAY BE IN YOUR SWING PATH.....

TO CHECK OBSERVE YOUR DIVOTS....

DIVOTS POINTING LEFT OF TARGET MEANS THAT THE CLUB WAS ALIGNED LEFT AT THE TOP CAUSING MOST PROBABLY, A SLICE.

CONVERSELY, IF THE SHAFT POINTS RIGHT AT THE TOP, THE DIVOT WILL RUN PARALLEL AND YOU'LL LIKELY HOOK THE BALL.

Move Weight with Club

I LIKE TO MOVE MY WEIGHT IN UNISON WITH THE CLUB DURING MY SWING. AT ADDRESS I DISTRIBUTE MY WEIGHT EVENLY BETWEEN BOTH FEET. AS THE CLUB MOVES INTO THE BACKSWING PERHAPS 80 PERCENT MOVES TO MY RIGHT SIDE. THE DOWN-SWING IS A MIRROR IMAGE. AT IMPACT PERHAPS 80 PER CENT OF MY WEIGHT IS ON MY LEFT SIDE.

50%   50%   80%   80%

Set-up with the Right Side Low

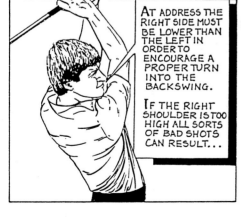

AT ADDRESS THE RIGHT SIDE MUST BE LOWER THAN THE LEFT IN ORDER TO ENCOURAGE A PROPER TURN INTO THE BACKSWING.

IF THE RIGHT SHOULDER IS TOO HIGH ALL SORTS OF BAD SHOTS CAN RESULT...

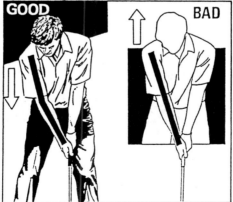

GOOD   BAD

SO, KEEP YOUR RIGHT ARM RELAXED AND BENT WITH THE RIGHT ELBOW SLIGHTLY TUCKED INTO THE SIDE.

A Smooth Takeaway

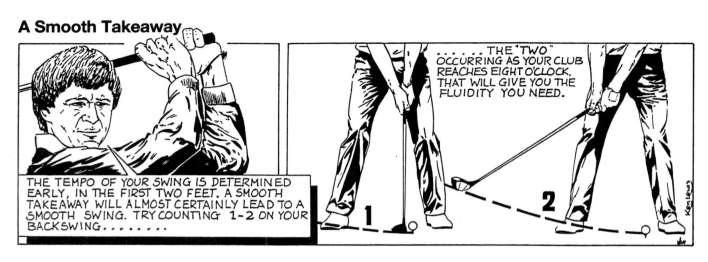

THE TEMPO OF YOUR SWING IS DETERMINED EARLY, IN THE FIRST TWO FEET. A SMOOTH TAKEAWAY WILL ALMOST CERTAINLY LEAD TO A SMOOTH SWING. TRY COUNTING 1-2 ON YOUR BACKSWING . . . .

. . . . . . THE "TWO" OCCURRING AS YOUR CLUB REACHES EIGHT O'CLOCK. THAT WILL GIVE YOU THE FLUIDITY YOU NEED.

1   **2**

Lift Right Toe at Address

AT THE TOP OF THE BACKSWING MOST OF YOUR WEIGHT SHOULD BE ON YOUR RIGHT HEEL. MAKE THIS MOVE EASIER BY LIFTING YOUR RIGHT TOE AT ADDRESS.

THAT WILL SHIFT YOUR WEIGHT ONTO YOUR HEEL AUTOMATICALLY, LEAVING YOU FREE TO CONCENTRATE ON MAKING A SMOOTH TAKEAWAY.

Turn out both Feet

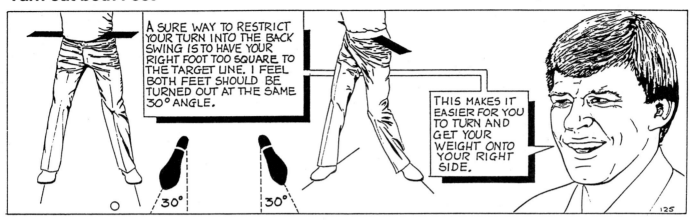

A SURE WAY TO RESTRICT YOUR TURN INTO THE BACK SWING IS TO HAVE YOUR RIGHT FOOT TOO SQUARE TO THE TARGET LINE. I FEEL BOTH FEET SHOULD BE TURNED OUT AT THE SAME 30° ANGLE.

30° 30°

THIS MAKES IT EASIER FOR YOU TO TURN AND GET YOUR WEIGHT ONTO YOUR RIGHT SIDE.

My Left Heel

A COMMON QUESTION ASKED BY GOLFERS IS: "HOW FAR SHOULD I LIFT MY LEFT HEEL ON THE BACKSWING?" WELL THE SIMPLE ANSWER IS: "AS FAR AS NECESSARY." . . . . .

. . . CONCENTRATE ON MAKING A TURN (UNTIL THE LEFT SHOULDER TOUCHES YOUR CHIN) AND HOW YOUR HEEL RISES WILL BE DETERMINED NATURALLY BY YOUR OWN LEVEL OF SUPPLENESS.

The More the Heavier

JUST HOW HIGH SHOULD THE LEFT HEEL RISE ON THE BACKSWING?

TO ME, THERE IS NO HARD AND FAST RULE. BUT, GENERALLY SPEAKING, A HEAVY SET PERSON SHOULD REQUIRE TO LIFT HIS LEFT HEEL A LOT MORE THAN SOMEONE WHO IS LIGHTER BUILT AND FAIRLY FLEXIBLE.

Turn to Eight O'Clock

I SPEND A LOT OF TIME WORKING ON MY FIRST MOVE INTO THE BACKSWING. AND SO SHOULD YOU. TRY THIS DRILL. PLACE THE BUTT OF YOUR CLUB IN YOUR NAVEL THEN TURN UNTIL THE SHAFT IS POINTING AT EIGHT O'CLOCK THAT IS THE PERFECT POSITION: THE CLUB IS ON PLANE AND YOUR BODY HAS BEGUN ITS TURN.

Count on the Backswing

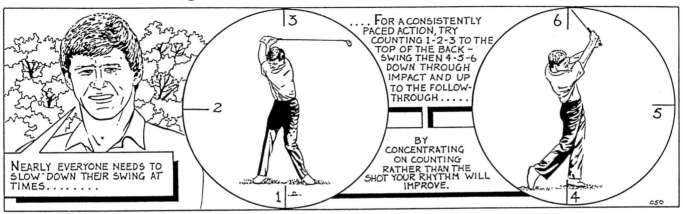

NEARLY EVERYONE NEEDS TO SLOW DOWN THEIR SWING AT TIMES........

.... FOR A CONSISTENTLY PACED ACTION, TRY COUNTING 1-2-3 TO THE TOP OF THE BACK-SWING THEN 4-5-6 DOWN THROUGH IMPACT AND UP TO THE FOLLOW-THROUGH.....

BY CONCENTRATING ON COUNTING RATHER THAN THE SHOT YOUR RHYTHM WILL IMPROVE.

Retain Right Knee Position

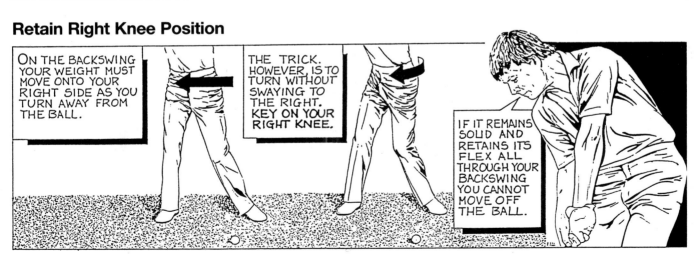

ON THE BACKSWING YOUR WEIGHT MUST MOVE ONTO YOUR RIGHT SIDE AS YOU TURN AWAY FROM THE BALL.

THE TRICK, HOWEVER, IS TO TURN WITHOUT SWAYING TO THE RIGHT. KEY ON YOUR RIGHT KNEE.

IF IT REMAINS SOLID AND RETAINS ITS FLEX ALL THROUGH YOUR BACKSWING YOU CANNOT MOVE OFF THE BALL.

Sometimes
you've got to grit your teeth

Swing Low and Smooth

A DECENT PASS AT THE BALL IS ONLY POSSIBLE AFTER A FLUID BACKSWING. SMOOTHNESS IS ALL IMPORTANT. FROM ADDRESS, KEEP YOUR LEFT ARM STRAIGHT, PUSH THE CLUB AWAY LOW, AND ∴ ALLOW YOUR WEIGHT TO SHIFT ON TO THE INSIDE OF YOUR RIGHT FOOT....

LOW

YES

NO

CONSCIOUS COCKING OF THE WRISTS IS UNNECESSARY, BUT DO NOT LET THEM GO PAST 90° AT THE TOP.

Exert Knee Pressure

A SWAY TO THE RIGHT ON THE BACKSWING IS OFTEN CAUSED BY A 'COLLAPSE' OF THE RIGHT KNEE.....

....TO AVOID THIS BE CONSCIOUS OF EXERTING A LITTLE MORE DOWNWARD PRESSURE THROUGH YOUR KNEE AND MAINTAIN THAT FEELING TO THE TOP OF YOUR BACKSWING.....

...IF YOUR KNEE DOESN'T MOVE TO THE RIGHT THEN YOUR HEAD CAN'T EITHER.

Keep Leg Action in Tune

LACK OF PROPER LEG ACTION WITHIN THE SWING CAN NEARLY ALWAYS BE TRACED BACK TO THE TAKEAWAY....

WHEN THE CLUB IS 'PICKED UP' ON TOO STEEP AN ARC THEN THE UPPER BODY WILL TAKE OVER, LEAVING THE LEG'S BEHIND....

IF YOU HAVE THIS PROBLEM, REHEARSE A SLOW, WIDE TAKEAWAY SO THAT YOUR LEGS MOVE IN TUNE WITH THE CLUB.

NARROW

STEEP

WIDE

SLOW

Too Far Too Bad

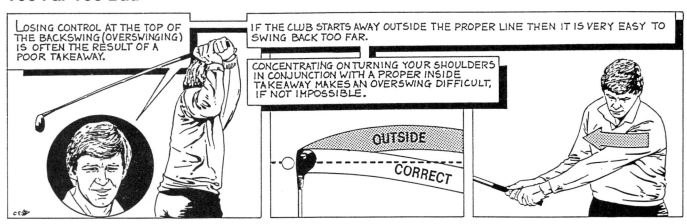

LOSING CONTROL AT THE TOP OF THE BACKSWING (OVERSWINGING) IS OFTEN THE RESULT OF A POOR TAKEAWAY.

IF THE CLUB STARTS AWAY OUTSIDE THE PROPER LINE THEN IT IS VERY EASY TO SWING BACK TOO FAR.

CONCENTRATING ON TURNING YOUR SHOULDERS IN CONJUNCTION WITH A PROPER INSIDE TAKEAWAY MAKES AN OVERSWING DIFFICULT, IF NOT IMPOSSIBLE.

OUTSIDE

CORRECT

At the Top

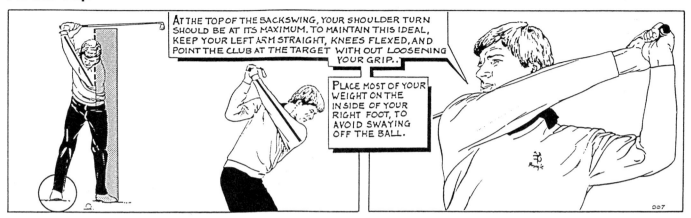

At the top of the backswing, your shoulder turn should be at its maximum. To maintain this ideal, keep your left arm straight, knees flexed, and point the club at the target without loosening your grip..

Place most of your weight on the inside of your right foot, to avoid swaying off the ball.

Turn the Body

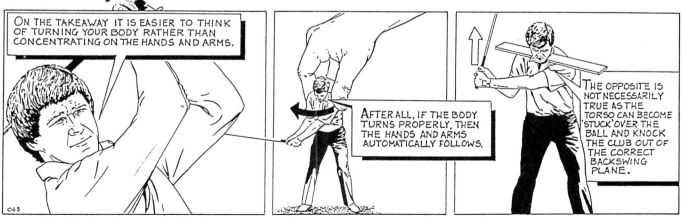

On the takeaway it is easier to think of turning your body rather than concentrating on the hands and arms.

After all, if the body turns properly, then the hands and arms automatically follows.

The opposite is not necessarily true as the torso can become 'stuck' over the ball and knock the club out of the correct backswing plane.

No slide on the Downswing

NO

YES

STARTING THE DOWNSWING PROPERLY IS ONE OF THE MOST IMPORTANT MOVES IN GOLF.
FROM THE TOP, THE CORRECT SEQUENCE OF EVENTS IS INITIATED BY SHIFT OF WEIGHT ON TO THE INSIDE OF THE LEFT FOOT. THIS IS VITAL, AS A LATERAL SLIDE OF THE KNEES TO THE LEFT MAKES IT VERY DIFFICULT TO REMAIN 'CENTRED' OVER THE BALL.

Collect the Ball

THINK OF YOUR SWING AS JUST THAT — A SWING. IMAGINE YOUR HITTING AREA AS BEING EIGHTEEN INCHES EITHER SIDE OF THE BALL.

YOUR AIM SHOULD BE TO SIMPLY HAVE YOUR CLUB COLLECT THE BALL AS IT PASSES. THERE SHOULD BE LITTLE OR NO SENSATION OF YOU HITTING AT THE BALL.

The Downswing

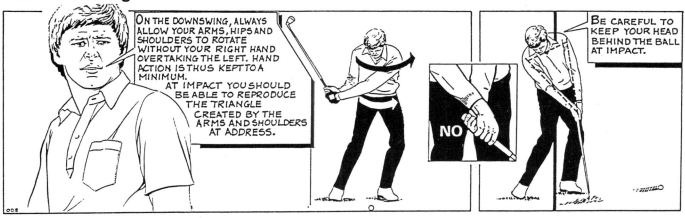

On the downswing, always allow your arms, hips and shoulders to rotate without your right hand overtaking the left. Hand action is thus kept to a minimum.

At impact you should be able to reproduce the triangle created by the arms and shoulders at address.

NO

Be careful to keep your head behind the ball at impact.

The Follow Through

I have heard golfers ask "Why bother with the swing after the ball has gone." But the follow through should not be neglected.......

Try to make the clubhead follow the ball, this will ensure that the swing has been made from the inside......

At the finish the follow through should resemble the top of the backswing, only in reverse.

Swing at 80 Per Cent

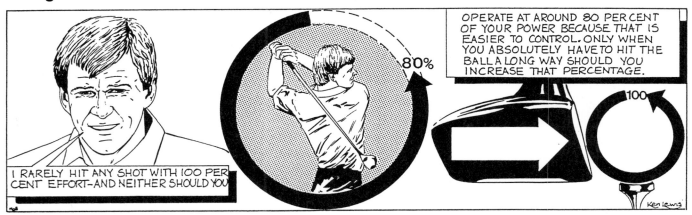

I RARELY HIT ANY SHOT WITH 100 PER CENT EFFORT—AND NEITHER SHOULD YOU.

80%

OPERATE AT AROUND 80 PER CENT OF YOUR POWER BECAUSE THAT IS EASIER TO CONTROL. ONLY WHEN YOU ABSOLUTELY HAVE TO HIT THE BALL A LONG WAY SHOULD YOU INCREASE THAT PERCENTAGE.

100

Ken Lewis

Cure Your Hit From the Top

A COMMON FAULT IN GOLF IS HITTING "FROM THE TOP". TO MAKE SURE YOU DO NOT FALL INTO THIS TRAP, FOCUS ON YOUR LEFT SHOULDER. IF IT MOVES UP AND TO YOUR LEFT AT THE START OF YOUR DOWNSWING, YOUR ARMS MUST COME DOWN.

ANY INCLINATION TO HIT IS THUS DELAYED UNTIL LATER IN THE SWING.

THERE IS NOTHING MORE FRUSTRATING THAN WATCHING SOMEONE LOSING DISTANCE BY TRYING TO 'STEER' THE BALL. PROPER RELEASE OF THE CLUB CAN ONLY BE ACHIEVED BY A FREE UNINHIBITED SWING – SO DON'T HOLD BACK.

USE YOUR PRACTICE SWING AS A REHEARSAL AND TRY TO 'SWISH' THE CLUB THROUGH IMPACT.

SWISH

Don't Hold Back

WHEN YOUR SWING LOSES RHYTHM THE PROBLEM CAN OFTEN BE CAUSED BY EXCESS MOVEMENT IN ITS BASE – THE LEGS. TRY WIDENING THE STANCE AND IMAGINING MORE 'STABILITY' IN YOUR KNEES . . . .

THIS WILL HELP YOU MAKE A WELL-PACED SWING BY ELIMINATING MUCH OF THAT UNNECESSARY LEG WORK.

A Sound Base

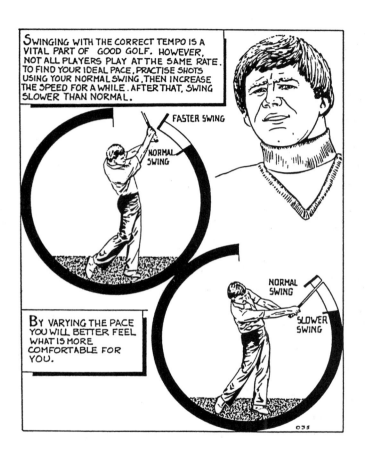

Swinging with the correct tempo is a vital part of good golf. However, not all players play at the same rate. To find your ideal pace, practise shots using your normal swing, then increase the speed for a while. After that, swing slower than normal.

FASTER SWING

NORMAL SWING

By varying the pace you will better feel what is more comfortable for you.

NORMAL SWING

SLOWER SWING

Find Your Pace

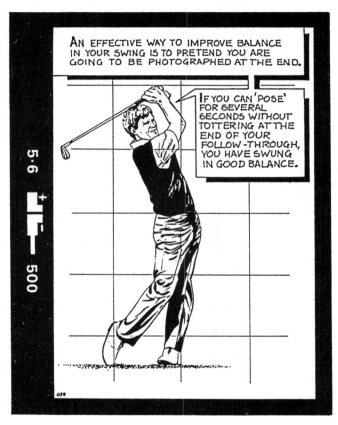

An effective way to improve balance in your swing is to pretend you are going to be photographed at the end.

If you can 'pose' for several seconds without tottering at the end of your follow-through, you have swung in good balance.

5·6

500

Improve your Balance

Putting on the style

ALMOST ALL OF TODAYS PROS USE AN ARM AND SHOULDER PUTTING STROKE WITH LITTLE HAND OR WRIST ACTION.....

TO MAKE THIS WORK YOU MUST HAVE A NARROW STANCE WHICH ALLOWS THE ARMS AND SHOULDERS SUFFICIENT FREEDOM TO SWING THE PUTTER......

TOO WIDE A STANCE RESTRICTS ARM AND SHOULDER MOVEMENT AND ENCOURAGES HAND/WRIST INVOLVEMENT IN THE STROKE.

Putting Stance

42

Start on Line

HAVING TROUBLE STARTING YOUR YOUR PUTTS ON-LINE? IT COULD BE THAT YOUR FOREARMS ARE MIS-ALIGNED. MOST COMMONLY, PLAYERS ALLOW THEIR RIGHT FOREARM TO GET HIGHER THAN THE LEFT SO THAT THEY ARE AIMING WELL LEFT OF THE HOLE.....

TO PREVENT THIS, FEEL THAT YOUR RIGHT ELBOW IS "TUCKED-IN" TO YOUR SIDE AND WATCH THOSE PUTTS GO IN!

Don't Watch the Putter Head

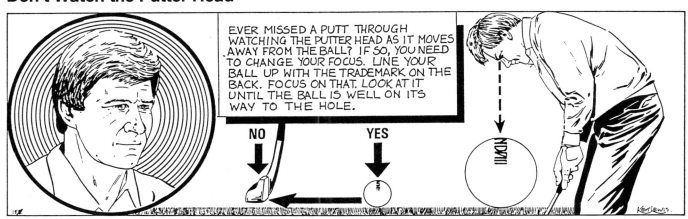

EVER MISSED A PUTT THROUGH WATCHING THE PUTTER HEAD AS IT MOVES AWAY FROM THE BALL? IF SO, YOU NEED TO CHANGE YOUR FOCUS. LINE YOUR BALL UP WITH THE TRADEMARK ON THE BACK. FOCUS ON THAT. LOOK AT IT UNTIL THE BALL IS WELL ON ITS WAY TO THE HOLE.

NO   YES

Putt with your Eyes Closed

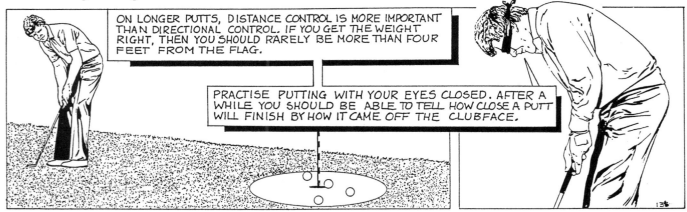

ON LONGER PUTTS, DISTANCE CONTROL IS MORE IMPORTANT THAN DIRECTIONAL CONTROL. IF YOU GET THE WEIGHT RIGHT, THEN YOU SHOULD RARELY BE MORE THAN FOUR FEET FROM THE FLAG.

PRACTISE PUTTING WITH YOUR EYES CLOSED. AFTER A WHILE YOU SHOULD BE ABLE TO TELL HOW CLOSE A PUTT WILL FINISH BY HOW IT CAME OFF THE CLUBFACE.

Stay over the Ball

EXTRANEOUS BODY MOVEMENT USUALLY SPELLS DISASTER ON THE PUTTING GREEN.

IT IS IMPERATIVE THAT ONLY YOUR HANDS, ARMS AND SHOULDERS ARE INVOLVED IN THE STROKE.

TO MAKE SURE I STAY STILL OVER THE BALL. I "HIT AND LISTEN." ONLY AFTER I HEAR THE BALL HIT THE CUP DO I ALLOW MY HEAD TO COME UP.

CLUNK

Swing, Don't Scrape

IT IS DIFFICULT TO HIT PUTTS WELL IF YOUR STROKE IS JERKY RATHER THAN SMOOTH. I LIKE TO BEGIN MY STROKE WITH THE PUTTER HEAD A LITTLE OFF THE GROUND. THAT GETS ME OFF TO A CONSISTENT START, THERE BEING NO DANGER OF MY SCRAPING THE CLUB ALONG THE GROUND KNOCKING IT OFF LINE.

Focus on the Right Elbow

FOSTER THIS BY STROKING SOME PUTTS WITH YOUR RIGHT HAND ONLY. THIS WILL HELP YOU MAINTAIN A CLOSE RELATIONSHIP BETWEEN YOUR ELBOW AND HIP.

A COMMON FACTOR IN EVERY GOOD PUTTING STROKE IS THE POSITION OF THE RIGHT ELBOW IT NEVER MOVES TOO FAR AWAY FROM THE RIGHT HIP.

Pick a Line – and Stick to it

ON THE GREEN YOUR FIRST THOUGHTS ARE INVARIABLY YOUR BEST. ONCE YOU HAVE DECIDED ON THE LINE OF A PUTT, NEVER *SECOND GUESS* YOURSELF.

?

FIRST THOUGHTS

SMOOTH

SOLID...

A SMOOTH STROKE AND A SOLID CONTACT BETWEEN CLUB AND BALL ARE MORE EASILY ATTAINED WHEN YOUR MIND IS CLEAR OF INDECISIONS.

Side Becomes Front

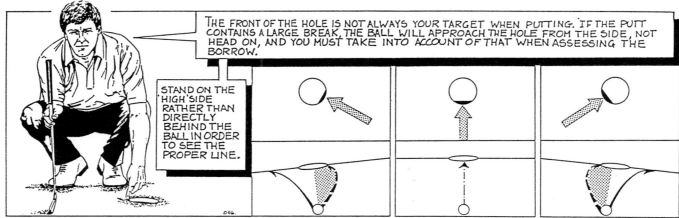

THE FRONT OF THE HOLE IS NOT ALWAYS YOUR TARGET WHEN PUTTING. IF THE PUTT CONTAINS A LARGE BREAK, THE BALL WILL APPROACH THE HOLE FROM THE SIDE, NOT HEAD ON, AND YOU MUST TAKE INTO ACCOUNT OF THAT WHEN ASSESSING THE BORROW.

STAND ON THE HIGH SIDE RATHER THAN DIRECTLY BEHIND THE BALL IN ORDER TO SEE THE PROPER LINE.

Low and Slow

MISSING TOO MANY PUTTS ON THE LEFT? THEN YOU ARE PROBABLY 'PICKING UP THE CLUB' ON THE BACKSWING.

ALMOST EVERY GOOD PUTTER TAKES THE CLUB AWAY FROM THE BALL LOW AND SLOW SO CONCENTRATE ON THAT AND WATCH THOSE PUTTS FALL!

TOO STEEP

NO

YES

Long Better than Short

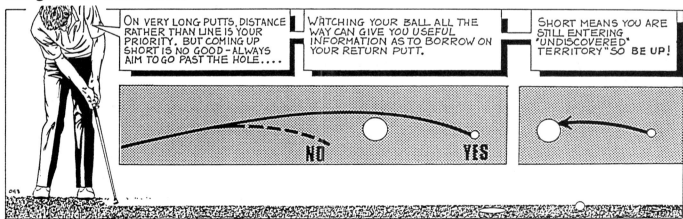

ON VERY LONG PUTTS, DISTANCE RATHER THAN LINE IS YOUR PRIORITY. BUT COMING UP SHORT IS NO GOOD - ALWAYS AIM TO GO PAST THE HOLE....

WATCHING YOUR BALL ALL THE WAY CAN GIVE YOU USEFUL INFORMATION AS TO BORROW ON YOUR RETURN PUTT.

SHORT MEANS YOU ARE STILL ENTERING "UNDISCOVERED" TERRITORY "SO BE UP!

NO

YES

Half of the Game

WE ALL KNOW HOW MUCH FUN IT IS TO STAND ON THE PRACTICE GROUND HITTING DRIVER AFTER DRIVER. HOWEVER, THIS IS NO WAY TO IMPROVE YOUR SCORING IN THE LONG-RUN.....

IT IS MUCH MORE PRODUCTIVE TO SPEND THE MAJORITY OF YOUR PRACTICE TIME CHIPPING AND PUTTING...

REMEMBER, PUTTING ALONE IS 'HALF THE GAME'

Straight Putts

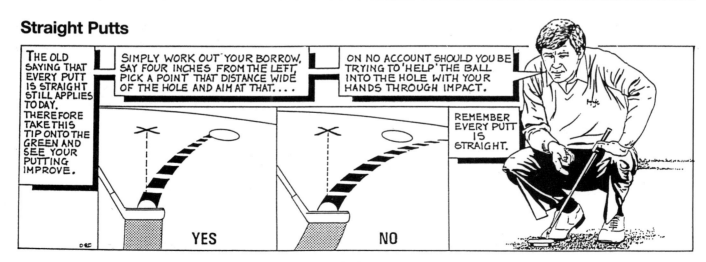

THE OLD SAYING THAT EVERY PUTT IS STRAIGHT STILL APPLIES TODAY. THEREFORE TAKE THIS TIP ONTO THE GREEN AND SEE YOUR PUTTING IMPROVE.

SIMPLY WORK OUT YOUR BORROW, SAY FOUR INCHES FROM THE LEFT, PICK A POINT THAT DISTANCE WIDE OF THE HOLE AND AIM AT THAT....

ON NO ACCOUNT SHOULD YOU BE TRYING TO 'HELP' THE BALL INTO THE HOLE WITH YOUR HANDS THROUGH IMPACT.

REMEMBER EVERY PUTT IS STRAIGHT.

YES

NO

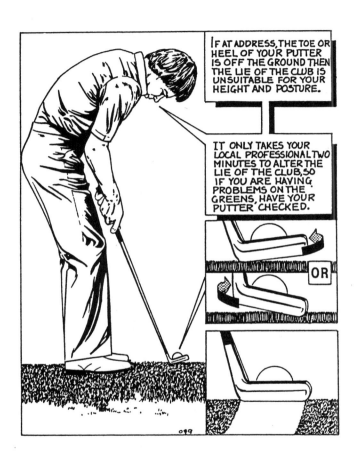

IF AT ADDRESS, THE TOE OR HEEL OF YOUR PUTTER IS OFF THE GROUND THEN THE LIE OF THE CLUB IS UNSUITABLE FOR YOUR HEIGHT AND POSTURE.

IT ONLY TAKES YOUR LOCAL PROFESSIONAL TWO MINUTES TO ALTER THE LIE OF THE CLUB, SO IF YOU ARE HAVING PROBLEMS ON THE GREENS, HAVE YOUR PUTTER CHECKED.

OR

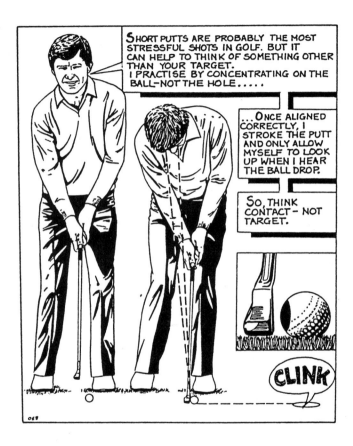

SHORT PUTTS ARE PROBABLY THE MOST STRESSFUL SHOTS IN GOLF. BUT IT CAN HELP TO THINK OF SOMETHING OTHER THAN YOUR TARGET. I PRACTISE BY CONCENTRATING ON THE BALL—NOT THE HOLE.....

...ONCE ALIGNED CORRECTLY, I STROKE THE PUTT AND ONLY ALLOW MYSELF TO LOOK UP WHEN I HEAR THE BALL DROP.

SO, THINK CONTACT — NOT TARGET.

CLINK

Knock your Putter into Shape

Concentrate on the Ball

ON WINDY DAYS EVERY SHOT IS DIFFICULT BUT MAINTAINING BALANCE ON THE PUTTING GREEN IS ALWAYS ONE OF THE BIGGEST PROBLEMS. USING A WIDER STANCE IS OFTEN ADVANCED AS A SOLUTION BUT I FEEL SUCH A MOVE AFFECTS MY STROKE MORE THAN NECESSARY.........

INSTEAD, I SIMPLY TURN THE TOES OF MY FEET OUTWARDS - THIS MINIMISES ANY CHANGE TO MY PUTTING ACTION.

WIND

Putting in the Wind

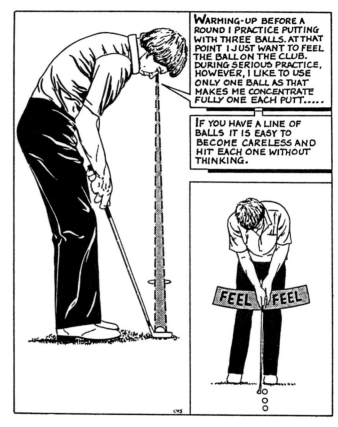

WARMING-UP BEFORE A ROUND I PRACTICE PUTTING WITH THREE BALLS. AT THAT POINT I JUST WANT TO FEEL THE BALL ON THE CLUB. DURING SERIOUS PRACTICE, HOWEVER, I LIKE TO USE ONLY ONE BALL AS THAT MAKES ME CONCENTRATE FULLY ON EACH PUTT.....

IF YOU HAVE A LINE OF BALLS IT IS EASY TO BECOME CARELESS AND HIT EACH ONE WITHOUT THINKING.

FEEL FEEL

Three – way Practice

Putt with a Wedge

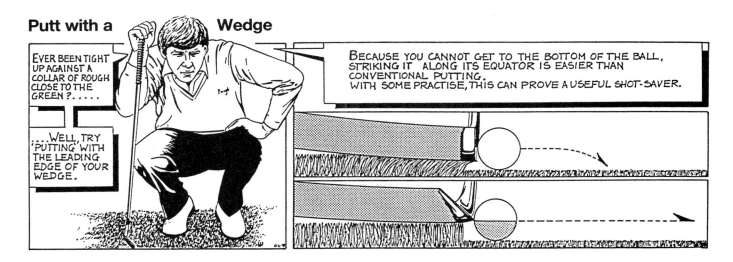

EVER BEEN TIGHT UP AGAINST A COLLAR OF ROUGH CLOSE TO THE GREEN ?.....

....WELL, TRY 'PUTTING' WITH THE LEADING EDGE OF YOUR WEDGE.

BECAUSE YOU CANNOT GET TO THE BOTTOM OF THE BALL, STRIKING IT ALONG ITS EQUATOR IS EASIER THAN CONVENTIONAL PUTTING.
WITH SOME PRACTISE, THIS CAN PROVE A USEFUL SHOT-SAVER.

Bellied Wedge

WHEN YOUR BALL IS UP AGAINST A COLLAR OF ROUGH JUST OFF THE GREEN, IT IS DIFFICULT TO MAKE AN EFFECTIVE CHIP. TRY THIS SHOT INSTEAD.

USING YOUR PUTTER GRIP TAKE YOUR WEDGE AND ADDRESS THE BALL ALONG ITS EQUATOR THEN MAKE A NORMAL PUTTING STROKE HITTING THE BALL HALF WAY UP. IT SHOULD COME OUT ROLLING, JUST LIKE A PUTT.

*'Squeeze' the ball at impact –
and follow through.*

Squeeze and Through

If you have trouble with a 'scooping' action on your chips, try moving the ball back in your stance to encourage a crisper strike. Maintain the triangle formed by the shoulders and arms, and using little wrist action, "squeeze" the ball at impact. Make sure also to follow-through — do not stop at the ball.

See the Shot

The next time you face a chip shot, imagine that it is just a putt. Take time to read any break or slope involved and aim just as precisely as you would on the greens.

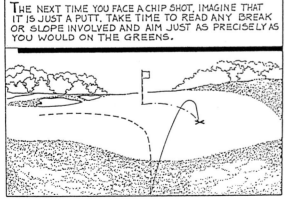

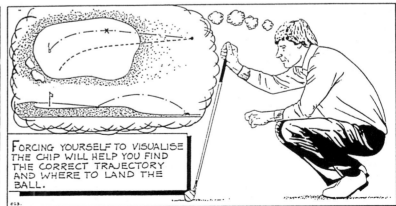

Forcing yourself to visualise the chip will help you find the correct trajectory and where to land the ball.

Take the Low Road

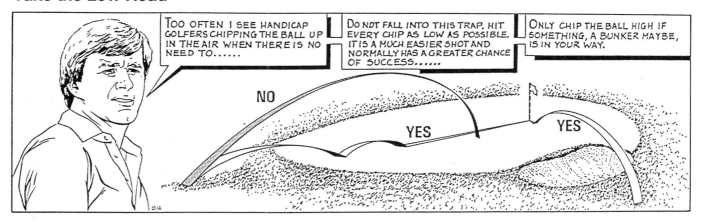

Chip from Heavy Rough

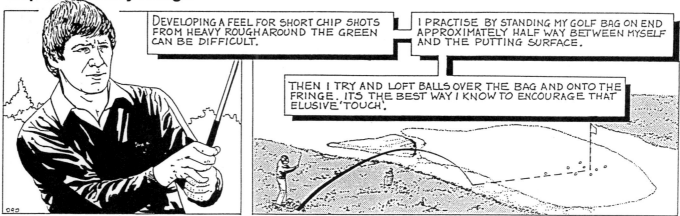

TOPPED CHIPS ARE NORMALLY CAUSED BY PANIC. THE PLAYER IS SO TENSE OVER THE BALL HIS WHOLE BODY MOVES UP DURING THE SWING.
BEAT THIS BY FOCUSING ON TAKING A TINY DIVOT AFTER THE SHOT.

THIS WILL ENCOURAGE THE PROPER 'SQUEEZE' OF THE BALL BETWEEN CLUB AND TURF AND ALSO KEEP YOUR HEAD STILL.

Don't Panic

Find the Flat Spots

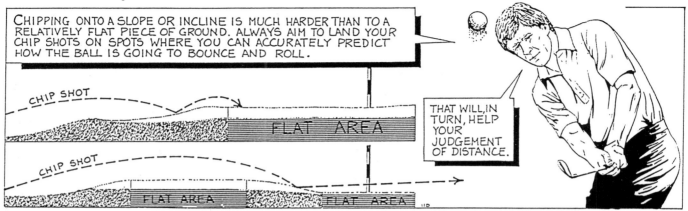

CHIPPING ONTO A SLOPE OR INCLINE IS MUCH HARDER THAN TO A RELATIVELY FLAT PIECE OF GROUND. ALWAYS AIM TO LAND YOUR CHIP SHOTS ON SPOTS WHERE YOU CAN ACCURATELY PREDICT HOW THE BALL IS GOING TO BOUNCE AND ROLL.

CHIP SHOT

FLAT AREA

CHIP SHOT

FLAT AREA

FLAT AREA

THAT WILL, IN TURN, HELP YOUR JUDGEMENT OF DISTANCE.

High or Low

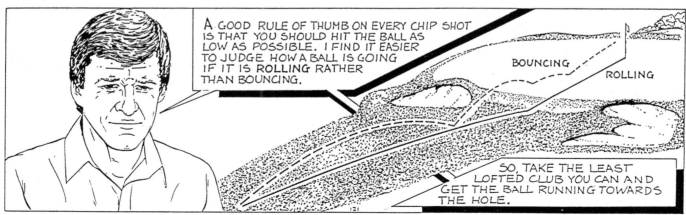

A GOOD RULE OF THUMB ON EVERY CHIP SHOT IS THAT YOU SHOULD HIT THE BALL AS LOW AS POSSIBLE. I FIND IT EASIER TO JUDGE HOW A BALL IS GOING IF IT IS ROLLING RATHER THAN BOUNCING.

BOUNCING

ROLLING

SO, TAKE THE LEAST LOFTED CLUB YOU CAN AND GET THE BALL RUNNING TOWARDS THE HOLE.

Hit Down on Chips

GOOD CHIP SHOTS RESULT FROM A CRISP DOWNWARD CONTACT BETWEEN CLUB AND BALL.

MAKE SURE YOU SET UP WITH YOUR WEIGHT FORWARD AND THE BALL A LITTLE BACK IN YOUR STANCE IN ORDER TO ENCOURAGE THAT DOWNWARD ARC.

With the Grass Against

GRASS LYING AGAINST THE DIRECTION IN WHICH YOU WANT THE BALL TO GO CAN MAKE CHIPPING VERY DIFFICULT.
TO ENCOURAGE THE DOWNWARD BLOW YOU NEED, PLACE A LITTLE MORE WEIGHT ON YOUR LEFT SIDE . . . .

. . . . . AND MOVE YOUR HANDS FARTHER AHEAD OF THE BALL. YOUR FOLLOW THROUGH SHOULD BE SHORTER THAN NORMAL.

Ken Lewis

Uphill Chip

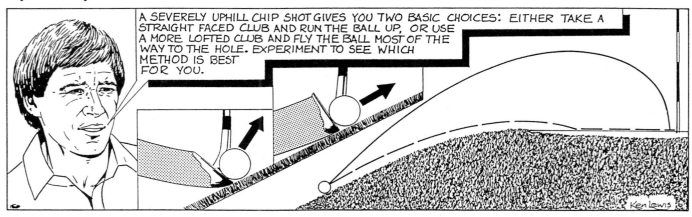

A SEVERELY UPHILL CHIP SHOT GIVES YOU TWO BASIC CHOICES: EITHER TAKE A STRAIGHT FACED CLUB AND RUN THE BALL UP, OR USE A MORE LOFTED CLUB AND FLY THE BALL MOST OF THE WAY TO THE HOLE. EXPERIMENT TO SEE WHICH METHOD IS BEST FOR YOU.

Ken Lewis

It's not too difficult
to avoid a Sand Storm

Square Aim, Open Stance

YOUR FEET ALIGNED TO THE LEFT. THEN SWING ALONG THE LINE OF YOUR TOES,

BUNKERS CAUSE THE HANDICAP GOLFER MORE PROBLEMS THAN THEY SHOULD. KEEP THINGS SIMPLE. AIM THE CLUBFACE AT THE HOLE, BUT STAND OPEN,

HITTING THE SAND AROUND TWO INCHES BEHIND THE BALL. FOLLOW THROUGH, AND THE BALL SHOULD POP OUT EVERY TIME.

Stay Steady

SWINGING TOO HARD IS THE CAUSE OF MANY BAD SHOTS FROM FAIRWAY BUNKERS. IF YOUR FEET SLIP IN THE SAND THE WHOLE SWING IS THROWN OFF BALANCE.......

HARD TAKEAWAY

TRY TO RESTRICT YOUR LEG MOVEMENT AS THIS WILL HAVE THE EFFECT OF SHORTENING YOUR SWING AND IN TURN, HELP KEEP YOU STEADY OVER THE BALL.

Long Bunker Shot

TOO FAR FOR AN EXPLOSION BUT NOT LONG ENOUGH FOR A FULL SWING, THE 50-YARD BUNKER SHOT IS A PROBLEM EVEN FOR PROFESSIONALS.

TARGET AREA

50 YDS

...THE SWING MUST BE DOMINATED BY THE HANDS AND ARMS - USE VERY LITTLE BODY MOVEMENT - BUT YOUR "FEEL" FOR THE SHOT IS MOST IMPORTANT. DO NOT SET YOUR SIGHTS TOO HIGH - SETTLE FOR HITTING THE GREEN.

The Short Explosion

WHEN FACED WITH A VERY SHORT EXPLOSION FROM A BUNKER I LIKE TO MOVE THE BALL BACK IN MY STANCE A FRACTION........

.... COCK MY WRISTS A LITTLE MORE THAN NORMAL AND MAKE A SHORT, POSITIVE SWING. AS LONG AS I FOLLOW THROUGH THERE IS LITTLE CHANCE OF ME LEAVING THE BALL IN THE TRAP.

From Hard Sand

PLAYING A BUNKER SHOT FROM CLOSELY-PACKED SAND IS NOT AS FEARSOME AS YOU MIGHT THINK

OPEN THE FACE OF YOUR SAND-WEDGE AS NORMAL BUT HIT 'DOWN' THROUGH THE SHOT EVEN MORE THAN USUAL.

BECAUSE THE CLUB WILL BOUNCE, DO NOT HIT TOO FAR BEHIND THE BALL - PERHAPS AN INCH IS ENOUGH.

TOO FAR BEHIND THE BALL FOR HARD SAND, BUT CORRECT FOR SOFT SAND

ENTRY POINT IS ABOUT ONE INCH BEHIND THE BALL IN HARD SAND

Adjust in Soft Sand

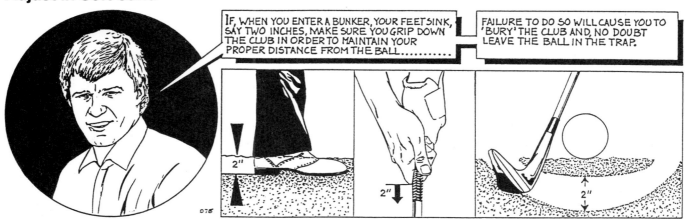

IF, WHEN YOU ENTER A BUNKER, YOUR FEET SINK, SAY TWO INCHES, MAKE SURE YOU GRIP DOWN THE CLUB IN ORDER TO MAINTAIN YOUR PROPER DISTANCE FROM THE BALL.............

FAILURE TO DO SO WILL CAUSE YOU TO 'BURY' THE CLUB AND, NO DOUBT LEAVE THE BALL IN THE TRAP.

2"

2"

2"

Cut Shot Over Bunkers

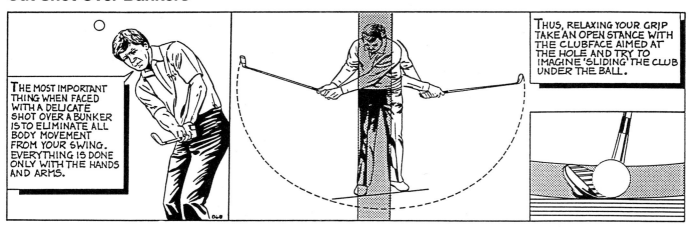

THE MOST IMPORTANT THING WHEN FACED WITH A DELICATE SHOT OVER A BUNKER IS TO ELIMINATE ALL BODY MOVEMENT FROM YOUR SWING. EVERYTHING IS DONE ONLY WITH THE HANDS AND ARMS.

THUS, RELAXING YOUR GRIP TAKE AN OPEN STANCE WITH THE CLUBFACE AIMED AT THE HOLE AND TRY TO IMAGINE 'SLIDING' THE CLUB UNDER THE BALL.

Chip from the Bunkers

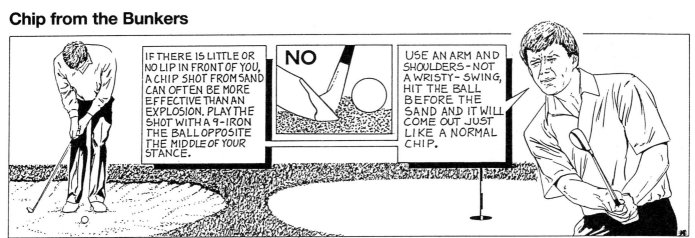

IF THERE IS LITTLE OR NO LIP IN FRONT OF YOU, A CHIP SHOT FROM SAND CAN OFTEN BE MORE EFFECTIVE THAN AN EXPLOSION. PLAY THE SHOT WITH A 9-IRON THE BALL OPPOSITE THE MIDDLE OF YOUR STANCE.

NO

USE AN ARM AND SHOULDERS - NOT A WRISTY - SWING, HIT THE BALL BEFORE THE SAND AND IT WILL COME OUT JUST LIKE A NORMAL CHIP.

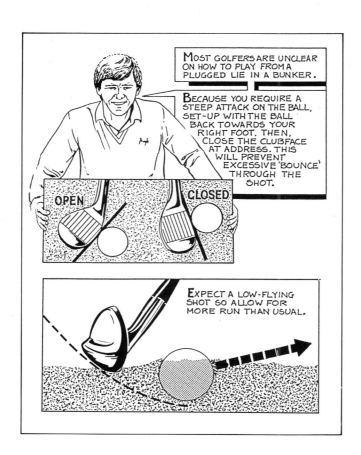

MOST GOLFERS ARE UNCLEAR ON HOW TO PLAY FROM A PLUGGED LIE IN A BUNKER.

BECAUSE YOU REQUIRE A STEEP ATTACK ON THE BALL, SET-UP WITH THE BALL BACK TOWARDS YOUR RIGHT FOOT. THEN, CLOSE THE CLUBFACE AT ADDRESS. THIS WILL PREVENT EXCESSIVE 'BOUNCE' THROUGH THE SHOT.

OPEN   CLOSED

EXPECT A LOW-FLYING SHOT SO ALLOW FOR MORE RUN THAN USUAL.

VERY SHORT BUNKER SHOTS ARE EASY IF YOUR TECHNIQUE IS SOUND.....

HOLD THE CLUB LIGHTLY - YOUR GRIP WILL TIGHTEN NATURALLY AS SOON AS YOU SWING - AND STAND 'OPEN' AT ADDRESS.......

THEN, KEEPING YOUR BODY VERY STILL, HIT AN INCH BEHIND THE BALL AND FEEL YOU ARE 'SLICING' UNDER THE BALL AND OUT OF THE SAND - FOLLOW - THROUGH ONLY A COUPLE OF FEET.

1 INCH

Plugged in Bunkers

Short Bunker Shots

Save yourself some grief
with a little thought

Remember how a good shot felt

WHEN EVER YOU HIT A PARTICULARLY GOOD SHOT, HOLD YOUR FOLLOW THROUGH LONGER THAN NORMAL.

CLOSE YOUR EYES, REMEMBER YOUR PRE-SHOT ROUTINE AND, MORE IMPORTANTLY HOW YOUR SWING FELT. THEN ATTEMPT TO REPEAT THE WHOLE PROCESS.

Be Confident

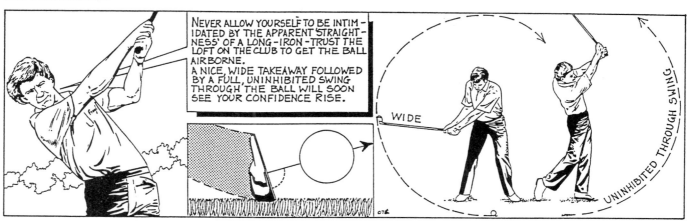

NEVER ALLOW YOURSELF TO BE INTIMIDATED BY THE APPARENT 'STRAIGHTNESS' OF A LONG-IRON-TRUST THE LOFT ON THE CLUB TO GET THE BALL AIRBORNE.
A NICE, WIDE TAKEAWAY FOLLOWED BY A FULL, UNINHIBITED SWING THROUGH THE BALL WILL SOON SEE YOUR CONFIDENCE RISE.

WIDE

UNINHIBITED THROUGH SWING

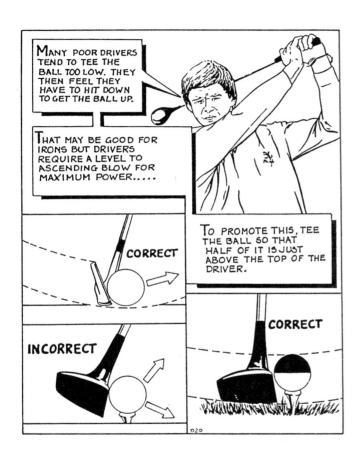

MANY POOR DRIVERS TEND TO TEE THE BALL TOO LOW. THEY THEN FEEL THEY HAVE TO HIT DOWN TO GET THE BALL UP.

THAT MAY BE GOOD FOR IRONS BUT DRIVERS REQUIRE A LEVEL TO ASCENDING BLOW FOR MAXIMUM POWER.....

CORRECT

TO PROMOTE THIS, TEE THE BALL SO THAT HALF OF IT IS JUST ABOVE THE TOP OF THE DRIVER.

INCORRECT

CORRECT

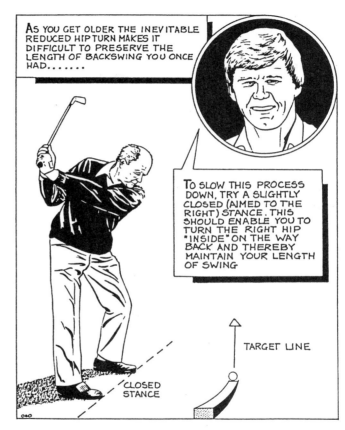

AS YOU GET OLDER THE INEVITABLE REDUCED HIP TURN MAKES IT DIFFICULT TO PRESERVE THE LENGTH OF BACKSWING YOU ONCE HAD.......

TO SLOW THIS PROCESS DOWN, TRY A SLIGHTLY CLOSED (AIMED TO THE RIGHT) STANCE. THIS SHOULD ENABLE YOU TO TURN THE RIGHT HIP "INSIDE" ON THE WAY BACK AND THEREBY MAINTAIN YOUR LENGTH OF SWING

TARGET LINE

CLOSED STANCE

Tee the Ball up

For Older Players

Stay 'Behind' the Shot

AT IMPACT YOUR HEAD SHOULD BE BEHIND AN IMAGINARY LINE DRAWN UP FROM THE BALL........

..TO ENCOURAGE THIS, AT ADDRESS FOCUS ON A POINT ON THE BACK OF THE BALL. ONLY ALLOW YOURSELF TO LOOK UP WHEN THE FOLLOW-THROUGH IS ALMOST COMPLETE AND THE BALL IS WELL ON ITS WAY.

If in Doubt

STANDING ON THE TEE OF A PARTICULARLY NARROW HOLE CAN BE INTIMIDATING, SO, IF YOU ARE UNDECIDED, USE A 1-IRON OR A 4-WOOD. THERE IS NO SHAME IN NOT HITTING A DRIVER.

AS LONG AS YOU CAN STILL REACH THE GREEN IN TWO, SWALLOW YOUR PRIDE AND GET THE BALL IN PLAY.

GOOD DRIVE

1 IRON

Hit Soft Under Pressure

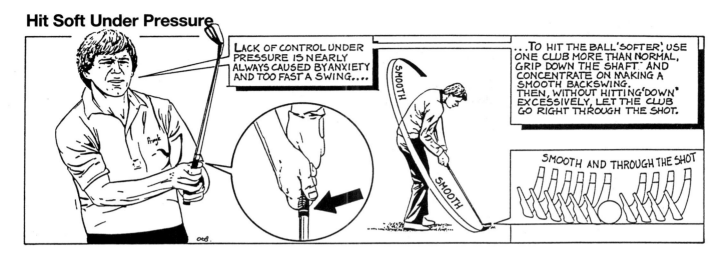

LACK OF CONTROL UNDER PRESSURE IS NEARLY ALWAYS CAUSED BY ANXIETY AND TOO FAST A SWING....

SMOOTH

SMOOTH

...TO HIT THE BALL 'SOFTER', USE ONE CLUB MORE THAN NORMAL, GRIP DOWN THE SHAFT AND CONCENTRATE ON MAKING A SMOOTH BACKSWING. THEN, WITHOUT HITTING 'DOWN' EXCESSIVELY, LET THE CLUB GO RIGHT THROUGH THE SHOT.

SMOOTH AND THROUGH THE SHOT

In the Cold

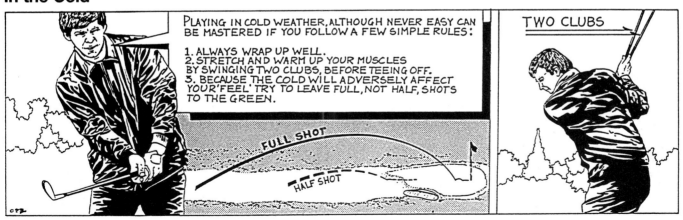

PLAYING IN COLD WEATHER, ALTHOUGH NEVER EASY CAN BE MASTERED IF YOU FOLLOW A FEW SIMPLE RULES:

1. ALWAYS WRAP UP WELL.
2. STRETCH AND WARM UP YOUR MUSCLES BY SWINGING TWO CLUBS, BEFORE TEEING OFF.
3. BECAUSE THE COLD WILL ADVERSELY AFFECT YOUR 'FEEL' TRY TO LEAVE FULL, NOT HALF, SHOTS TO THE GREEN.

FULL SHOT

HALF SHOT

TWO CLUBS

Hit 'Away' from Trouble

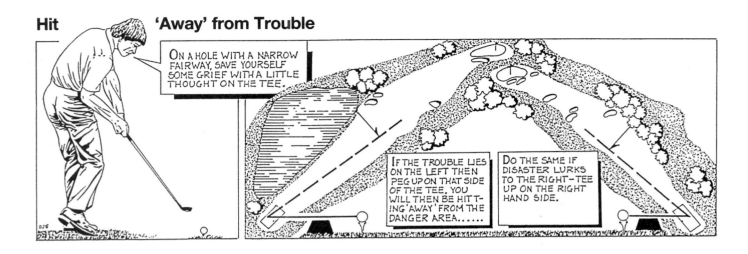

On a hole with a narrow fairway, save yourself some grief with a little thought on the tee.

If the trouble lies on the left then peg up on that side of the tee. You will then be hitting 'away' from the danger area......

Do the same if disaster lurks to the right—tee up on the right hand side.

Pitch Around the Clock

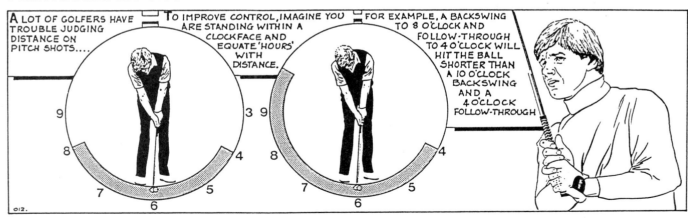

A lot of golfers have trouble judging distance on pitch shots....

To improve control, imagine you are standing within a clockface and equate 'hours' with distance.

For example, a backswing to 8 o'clock and follow-through to 4 o'clock will hit the ball shorter than a 10 o'clock backswing and a 4 o'clock follow-through

Hit the Ball High

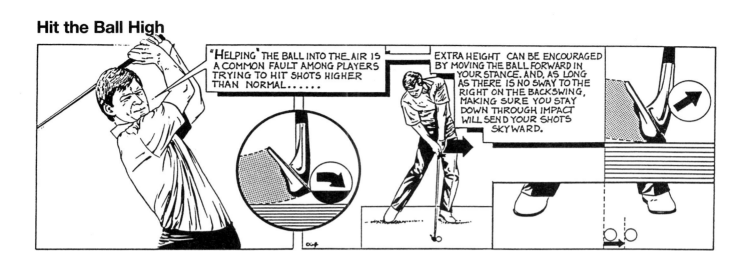

"HELPING" THE BALL INTO THE AIR IS A COMMON FAULT AMONG PLAYERS TRYING TO HIT SHOTS HIGHER THAN NORMAL......

EXTRA HEIGHT CAN BE ENCOURAGED BY MOVING THE BALL FORWARD IN YOUR STANCE. AND, AS LONG AS THERE IS NO SWAY TO THE RIGHT ON THE BACKSWING, MAKING SURE YOU STAY DOWN THROUGH IMPACT WILL SEND YOUR SHOTS SKYWARD.

Know your Distances

KNOWING HOW FAR YOU HIT EACH CLUB CAN KNOCK MANY SHOTS OFF YOUR SCORE.....

SO, NEXT TIME YOU ARE ON THE COURSE AND HIT WHAT YOU FEEL IS A GOOD SOLID SHOT, PACE OFF THE DISTANCE....

THAT WAY YOU WILL SOON HAVE AN ACCURATE GUIDE FOR EVERY CLUB.IN THE BAG.

DR 235+
3W 210
5W 200
3
4 178
5
6

7 143
8
9

Fairway Woods v Long Irons

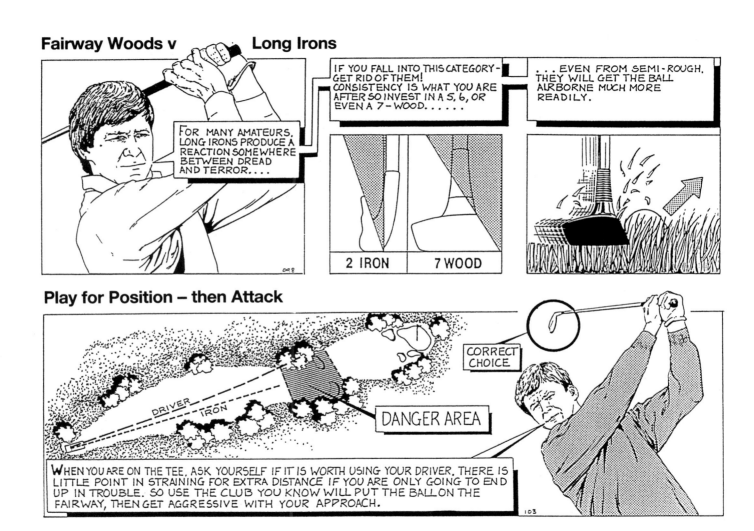

FOR MANY AMATEURS, LONG IRONS PRODUCE A REACTION SOMEWHERE BETWEEN DREAD AND TERROR....

IF YOU FALL INTO THIS CATEGORY - GET RID OF THEM! CONSISTENCY IS WHAT YOU ARE AFTER SO INVEST IN A 5, 6, OR EVEN A 7-WOOD......

... EVEN FROM SEMI-ROUGH. THEY WILL GET THE BALL AIRBORNE MUCH MORE READILY.

2 IRON

7 WOOD

Play for Position – then Attack

DRIVER

IRON

DANGER AREA

CORRECT CHOICE

WHEN YOU ARE ON THE TEE, ASK YOURSELF IF IT IS WORTH USING YOUR DRIVER. THERE IS LITTLE POINT IN STRAINING FOR EXTRA DISTANCE IF YOU ARE ONLY GOING TO END UP IN TROUBLE. SO USE THE CLUB YOU KNOW WILL PUT THE BALL ON THE FAIRWAY, THEN GET AGGRESSIVE WITH YOUR APPROACH.

One Shape is Best

THE HARDEST SHOT IN GOLF IS THE ONE THAT IS DEAD STRAIGHT.

THEREFORE IT IS A GOOD IDEA TO WORK ON MOVING THE BALL ONE WAY MOST OF THE TIME. IT DOES NOT MATTER IF YOU CHOOSE LEFT-TO-RIGHT OR RIGHT-TO-LEFT....

LEFT-TO-RIGHT

STRAIGHT

RIGHT TO LEFT

..BUT COMMIT YOURSELF TO ONE SHAPE AND IT IS MY GUESS YOU WILL HIT MORE FAIRWAYS AND GREENS.

Wider Stance for Half – Shots

WHEN YOU ARE PLAYING A SHOT AT LESS THAN FULL POWER, WIDEN YOUR STANCE. THIS WILL AUTOMATICALLY RESTRICT YOUR SWING - YOU DO NOT WANT THE CLUB TO TRAVEL MORE THAN SHOULDER HIGH. IT ALSO ALLOWS YOU TO HIT POSITIVELY THROUGH THE SHOT WITH NO FEAR OF IT FLYING TOO FAR.

Use Waggle as Rehearsal

BRISK AND FAST

A GOOD WAGGLE SHOULD ALWAYS BE A MINI-REHEARSAL FOR THE SHOT YOU ARE ABOUT TO PLAY. A **BRISK, FAST** WAGGLE WOULD BE APPOPRIATE WHEN YOU ARE USING A DRIVER, BUT IF YOU ARE FACED WITH A DELICATE CHIP OVER A BUNKER, YOUR WAGGLE SHOULD BE **SLOW AND SMOOTH**

SLOW AND SMOOTH

Read your Divots

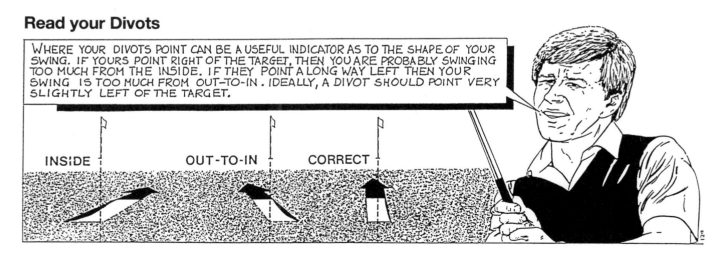

WHERE YOUR DIVOTS POINT CAN BE A USEFUL INDICATOR AS TO THE SHAPE OF YOUR SWING. IF YOURS POINT RIGHT OF THE TARGET, THEN YOU ARE PROBABLY SWINGING TOO MUCH FROM THE INSIDE. IF THEY POINT A LONG WAY LEFT THEN YOUR SWING IS TOO MUCH FROM OUT-TO-IN. IDEALLY, A DIVOT SHOULD POINT VERY SLIGHTLY LEFT OF THE TARGET.

INSIDE   OUT-TO-IN   CORRECT

Firm up your Left Wrist

TOO MUCH EMPHASIS ON A FIRM LEFT WRIST CAN CAUSE YOU TO LOSE THE SMOOTHNESS YOU NEED TO MAKE CONSISTENTLY GOOD PUTTS.

FOCUS INSTEAD ON MAINTAINING THE ANGLE AT THE BACK OF YOUR RIGHT WRIST ALL THROUGH THE STROKE. IF YOU DO THAT, THERE IS NO WAY YOUR LEFT WRIST CAN BREAK DOWN.

Hold your Follow Through

A LOT OF BAD SHOTS ARE CAUSED BY LOSS OF BALANCE. IF YOU HAVE TROUBLE IN THAT AREA, PRACTISE HOLDING YOUR FOLLOW THROUGH FOR UP TO FIVE SECONDS AFTER THE BALL HAS GONE. IF YOU CAN DO THIS WITHOUT FALLING OVER, THEN THE CHANCES ARE THAT YOU HAVE MADE A SMOOTH, BALANCED SWING.

15 Yards more from the Tee

90°

I WISH I HAD A POUND FOR EVERY TIME I HAVE SEEN A GOLFER THROW HIMSELF AT THE BALL IN AN ATTEMPT TO GET MORE DISTANCE. IF YOU NEED A BIG DRIVE..........

...FOCUS ON A FULL 90° DEGREE SHOULDER TURN AROUND A FIRM RIGHT KNEE ON THE BACKSWING. THEN SIMPLY UNWIND AS QUICKLY AS POSSIBLE ON THE DOWNSWING.

Hands Ahead of Clubhead

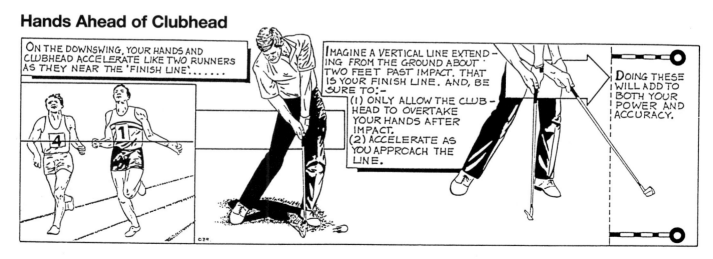

ON THE DOWNSWING, YOUR HANDS AND CLUBHEAD ACCELERATE LIKE TWO RUNNERS AS THEY NEAR THE 'FINISH LINE'.......

IMAGINE A VERTICAL LINE EXTENDING FROM THE GROUND ABOUT TWO FEET PAST IMPACT. THAT IS YOUR FINISH LINE. AND, BE SURE TO:-
(1) ONLY ALLOW THE CLUBHEAD TO OVERTAKE YOUR HANDS AFTER IMPACT.
(2) ACCELERATE AS YOU APPROACH THE LINE.

DOING THESE WILL ADD TO BOTH YOUR POWER AND ACCURACY.

Land Ball on the Green

I AM OFTEN ASKED IF I HAVE A FAVOURITE CHIPPING CLUB. I DON'T — NEITHER SHOULD YOU. CHIP WITH A VARIETY OF CLUBS. CHIP LOW WITH SAY, A 7-IRON; HIGH WITH A WEDGE. EITHER WAY, HOWEVER TRY TO LAND THE BALL ON THE GREEN, THAT GIVES YOU A BETTER FEEL FOR HOW FAR THE BALL WILL RUN.

WEDGE

7-IRON

Pin in Front get in Play

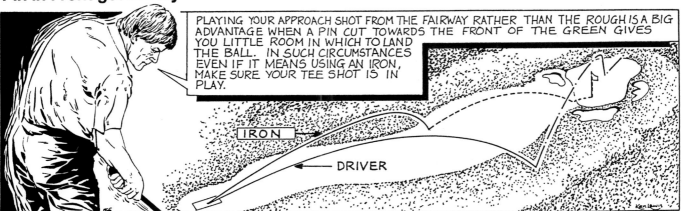

PLAYING YOUR APPROACH SHOT FROM THE FAIRWAY RATHER THAN THE ROUGH IS A BIG ADVANTAGE WHEN A PIN CUT TOWARDS THE FRONT OF THE GREEN GIVES YOU LITTLE ROOM IN WHICH TO LAND THE BALL. IN SUCH CIRCUMSTANCES EVEN IF IT MEANS USING AN IRON, MAKE SURE YOUR TEE SHOT IS IN PLAY.

IRON

DRIVER

Stay Calm for 18 Holes

NEVER FORGET THAT A ROUND LASTS 18 HOLES THERE IS NO POINT IN GETTING TOO EXCITED AT EARLY SUCCESS OR TOO DOWN IF YOU START BADLY. PLAY EACH SHOT ONE AT A TIME AND STAY ON THE SAME EMOTIONAL LEVEL ALL THE WAY TO THE 18th GREEN. BETTER SCORES WILL RESULT.

GOLF IS LIKE LIFE – FULL OF UPS AND DOWNS.

Set your own Par

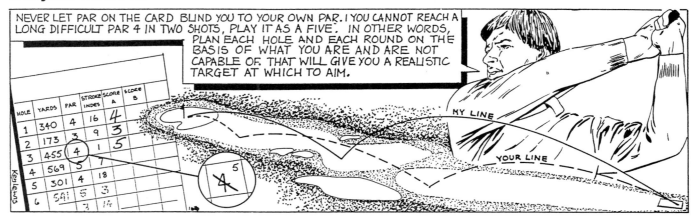

NEVER LET PAR ON THE CARD BLIND YOU TO YOUR OWN PAR. I YOU CANNOT REACH A LONG DIFFICULT PAR 4 IN TWO SHOTS, PLAY IT AS A FIVE. IN OTHER WORDS, PLAN EACH HOLE AND EACH ROUND ON THE BASIS OF WHAT YOU ARE AND ARE NOT CAPABLE OF. THAT WILL GIVE YOU A REALISTIC TARGET AT WHICH TO AIM.

MY LINE

YOUR LINE

Foursomes Tactics

IN THE 1987 RYDER CUP PLAYED AT MUIRFIELD VILLAGE, MY FOURSOMES PARTNER WAS IAN WOOSNAM.......

....BEFORE PLAYING WE PLOTTED OUR TACTICS. BECAUSE IAN HITS IRONS PARTICULARLY WELL, HE "TOOK" THE PAR-3'S. THIS MEANT I PLAYED ANY SHORT PITCHES ON THE PAR-5 HOLES.....

12th 156yds PAR 3

..THIS IS SOUND POLICY-ALWAYS AGREE WITH YOUR PARTNER WHICH HOLES OR SHOTS YOU WOULD LIKE.

5th 530yds PAR 5

Be a Match in Matchplay

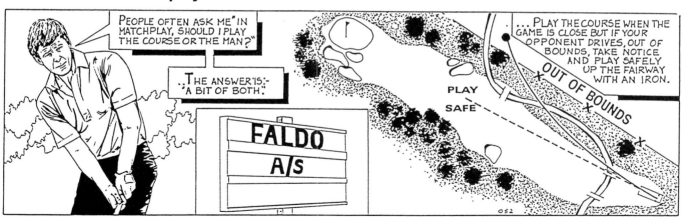

PEOPLE OFTEN ASK ME "IN MATCHPLAY, SHOULD I PLAY THE COURSE OR THE MAN?"

..THE ANSWER IS:- "A BIT OF BOTH".

FALDO
A/S

....PLAY THE COURSE WHEN THE GAME IS CLOSE BUT IF YOUR OPPONENT DRIVES, OUT OF BOUNDS, TAKE NOTICE AND PLAY SAFELY UP THE FAIRWAY WITH AN IRON.

PLAY SAFE

OUT OF BOUNDS

THE KEY TO SUCCESS IN FOURSOMES GOLF IS FINDING A PARTNER YOU LIKE PERSONALLY AND WHOSE GAME COMPLEMENTS YOURS....

IF YOU ARE, SAY, A GOOD DRIVER, PLAY WITH A FRIEND WHO IS A CONFIDENT IRON PLAYER..

.. AND, TALK TACTICS ON THE COURSE - ENCOURAGEMENT, PEP-TALKS AND HELP WITH THE LINES ON PUTTS, ALL AID TEAM SPIRIT.

The Perfect Partner

ON RAINY DAYS MAKE SURE YOU ARE SENSIBLY PREPARED OUT ON THE COURSE

IT IS NO USE BEMOANING YOUR LUCK IF YOU HAVE NOT BOTHERED TO CARRY:-
1. AN UMBRELLA.
2. GOLF BAG HEAD COVER.
3. TOWELS.
4. SPARE GLOVES.
5. WATERPROOFS.
PROPER PLANNING CAN SAVE YOU MANY SHOTS OVER 18 HOLES.

Get it Right in the Wet

Hands at Address

Anti-Hook Drill

Hook Around Trees

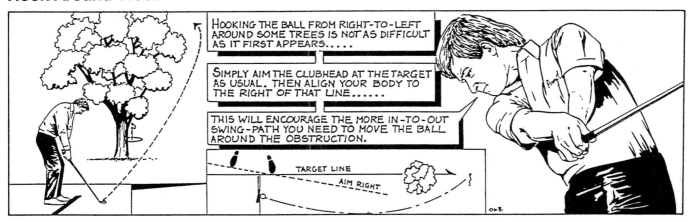

HOOKING THE BALL FROM RIGHT-TO-LEFT AROUND SOME TREES IS NOT AS DIFFICULT AS IT FIRST APPEARS.....

SIMPLY AIM THE CLUBHEAD AT THE TARGET AS USUAL. THEN ALIGN YOUR BODY TO THE RIGHT OF THAT LINE......

THIS WILL ENCOURAGE THE MORE IN-TO-OUT SWING-PATH YOU NEED TO MOVE THE BALL AROUND THE OBSTRUCTION.

TARGET LINE

AIM RIGHT

Divide by Four

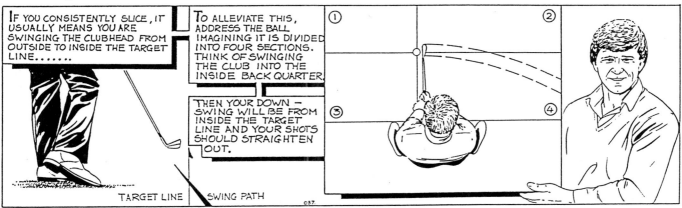

IF YOU CONSISTENTLY SLICE, IT USUALLY MEANS YOU ARE SWINGING THE CLUBHEAD FROM OUTSIDE TO INSIDE THE TARGET LINE.......

TO ALLEVIATE THIS, ADDRESS THE BALL IMAGINING IT IS DIVIDED INTO FOUR SECTIONS. THINK OF SWINGING THE CLUB INTO THE INSIDE BACK QUARTER.

THEN YOUR DOWN-SWING WILL BE FROM INSIDE THE TARGET LINE AND YOUR SHOTS SHOULD STRAIGHTEN OUT.

TARGET LINE

SWING PATH

① ② ③ ④

Turn Don't Slice

Deliberate Slice

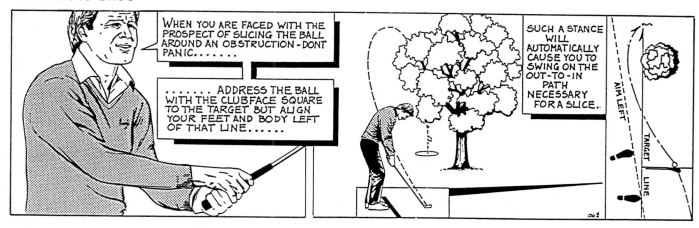

Up, up and away

Tee Higher or Lower in Wind

A COMMON MISTAKE I SEE IN MANY AMATEURS IS TEEING THE BALL LOW WHEN FACED WITH A DRIVE INTO THE WIND. TEE THE BALL UP HIGHER THAN NORMAL. THAT WILL ENCOURAGE THE CLUB TO APPROACH THE BALL ON THE SHALLOW ANGLE YOU NEED TO HIT A LOWER, MORE PENETRATING SHOT.

WIND

WIND

Narrow or Wide Stance

WIND

IF YOU WANT TO HIT THE BALL LOW INTO A STRONG WIND, TRY WIDENING YOUR STANCE. BY DOING SO, YOU RESTRICT YOUR LEG MOVEMENT AND BODY TURN.

THE RESULTING HANDS AND ARM DOMINATED SWING SEND THE BALL AWAY ON A LOWER TRAJECTORY.

Use the Wind Behind

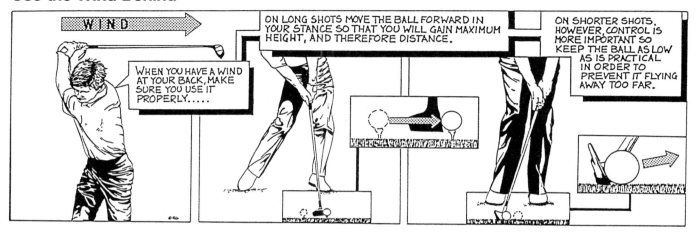

WIND

When you have a wind at your back, make sure you use it properly.....

ON LONG SHOTS MOVE THE BALL FORWARD IN YOUR STANCE SO THAT YOU WILL GAIN MAXIMUM HEIGHT, AND THEREFORE DISTANCE.

ON SHORTER SHOTS, HOWEVER, CONTROL IS MORE IMPORTANT SO KEEP THE BALL AS LOW AS IS PRACTICAL IN ORDER TO PREVENT IT FLYING AWAY TOO FAR.

Low Stroke Savers

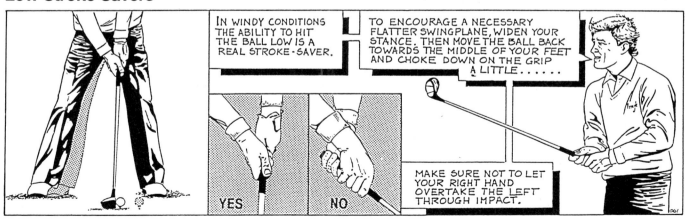

IN WINDY CONDITIONS THE ABILITY TO HIT THE BALL LOW IS A REAL STROKE-SAVER.

TO ENCOURAGE A NECESSARY FLATTER SWINGPLANE, WIDEN YOUR STANCE, THEN MOVE THE BALL BACK TOWARDS THE MIDDLE OF YOUR FEET AND CHOKE DOWN ON THE GRIP A LITTLE......

YES

NO

MAKE SURE NOT TO LET YOUR RIGHT HAND OVERTAKE THE LEFT THROUGH IMPACT.

Use, Don't Fight, The Wind

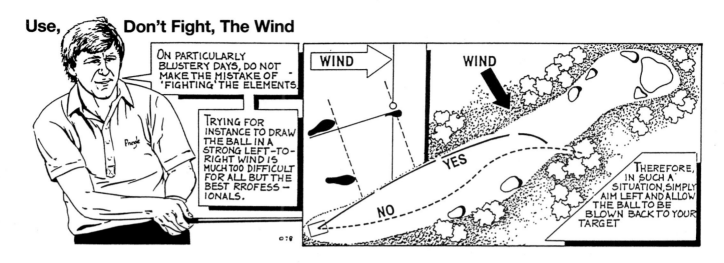

ON PARTICULARLY BLUSTERY DAYS, DO NOT MAKE THE MISTAKE OF 'FIGHTING' THE ELEMENTS.

TRYING FOR INSTANCE TO DRAW THE BALL IN A STRONG LEFT-TO-RIGHT WIND IS MUCH TOO DIFFICULT FOR ALL BUT THE BEST PROFESSIONALS.

WIND

WIND

YES

NO

THEREFORE, IN SUCH A SITUATION, SIMPLY AIM LEFT AND ALLOW THE BALL TO BE BLOWN BACK TO YOUR TARGET

Club Selection

ONE OF THE MOST COMMON WAYS OF SPOILING A SHOT IS INDECISION OVER CLUB SELECTION.

ONCE YOU HAVE TAKEN ALL FACTORS INTO ACCOUNT.....

.... LIE, WIND, DISTANCE, PIN POSITION – CHOOSE A CLUB AND STICK WITH IT...

ALLOWING DOUBTS TO ENTER YOUR MIND CAN ONLY DIVERT YOU FROM PLAYING AN AGGRESSIVE SHOT.

Taking the rough with the smooth

Playing from Rough

WHEN PLAYING FROM ROUGH, CHECK THE DIRECTION OF THE GRASS BEFORE DECIDING ON YOUR NEXT SHOT........

GRASS GROWING AWAY FROM THE TARGET WILL TEND TO GRAB AND CLOSE THE CLUBFACE SO TAKE MORE CLUB THAN NORMAL........

TAKE LESS CLUB WHEN THE REVERSE IS TRUE. A 'FLIER' CAN RESULT WHEN GRASS GROWING TOWARDS THE HOLE GETS BETWEEN CLUB AND BALL.

TARGET

Examining the Rough Lie

A CLOSE EXAMINATION OF YOUR LIE IN THE ROUGH CAN OFTEN HELP YOU IN YOUR CHOICE OF CLUB.

IF THE GRASS IS LYING TOWARDS THE TARGET, TAKE ONE CLUB **LESS**. THE BALL SHOULD RUN MORE ON LANDING.

GRASS LYING AWAY FROM THE HOLE CREATES MORE RESISTANCE AS YOU SWING THROUGH, SO TAKE AT LEAST ONE CLUB MORE.

FIRST CHOICE MINUS ONE CLUB

FIRST CHOICE PLUS ONE CLUB

Show Your Respect

I HAVE HEARD MANY PEOPLE SAY "MY 5-WOOD IS GREAT FROM THE ROUGH"

THAT MAY BE SO, BUT DO NOT BE TEMPTED INTO USING IT EVERY TIME. TREAT ROUGH WITH RESPECT AND MAKE SURE THAT THE CLUB USED WILL EASILY RETURN YOU TO THE FAIRWAY.

SAFETY ZONE

THAT IS RULE NUMBER ONE **GET THE BALL BACK IN PLAY.**

Taller Means Tighter

CONTROLLING A PITCH OR CHIP FROM HIGH GRASS IS ONE OF THE HARDEST SHOTS IN GOLF.......

TRYING TO PLACE THE CLUB DIRECTLY BEHIND THE BALL ONLY LEADS TO IT SNAGGING IN THE GRASS ON THE BACKSWING

SO ADDRESS THE BALL WITH THE CLUB ABOVE THE GRASS – A SMOOTH TAKEAWAY IS THEN MUCH EASIER.

I get by with a little help from my friends

Tight Lies

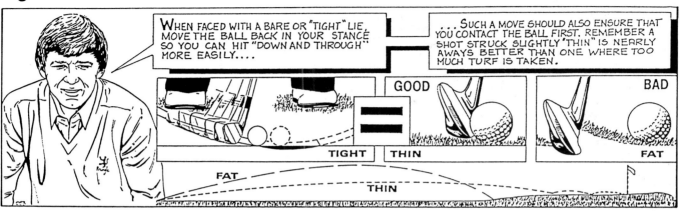

WHEN FACED WITH A BARE OR "TIGHT" LIE, MOVE THE BALL BACK IN YOUR STANCE SO YOU CAN HIT "DOWN AND THROUGH" MORE EASILY....

...SUCH A MOVE SHOULD ALSO ENSURE THAT YOU CONTACT THE BALL FIRST. REMEMBER A SHOT STRUCK SLIGHTLY "THIN" IS NEARLY ALWAYS BETTER THAN ONE WHERE TOO MUCH TURF IS TAKEN.

GOOD

BAD

TIGHT

THIN

FAT

FAT

THIN

The Half Wedge

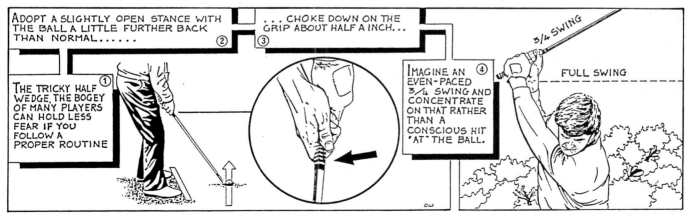

ADOPT A SLIGHTLY OPEN STANCE WITH THE BALL A LITTLE FURTHER BACK THAN NORMAL....... ②

...CHOKE DOWN ON THE GRIP ABOUT HALF A INCH... ③

THE TRICKY HALF WEDGE, THE BOGEY OF MANY PLAYERS CAN HOLD LESS FEAR IF YOU FOLLOW A PROPER ROUTINE ①

IMAGINE AN EVEN-PACED ¾ SWING AND CONCENTRATE ON THAT RATHER THAN A CONSCIOUS HIT "AT" THE BALL. ④

¾ SWING

FULL SWING

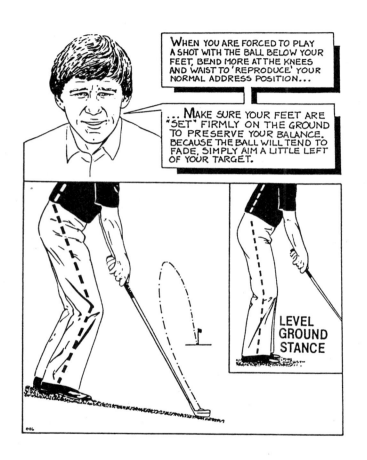

WHEN YOU ARE FORCED TO PLAY A SHOT WITH THE BALL BELOW YOUR FEET, BEND MORE AT THE KNEES AND WAIST TO 'REPRODUCE' YOUR NORMAL ADDRESS POSITION...

...MAKE SURE YOUR FEET ARE "SET" FIRMLY ON THE GROUND TO PRESERVE YOUR BALANCE. BECAUSE THE BALL WILL TEND TO FADE, SIMPLY AIM A LITTLE LEFT OF YOUR TARGET.

LEVEL GROUND STANCE

Ball Below Feet

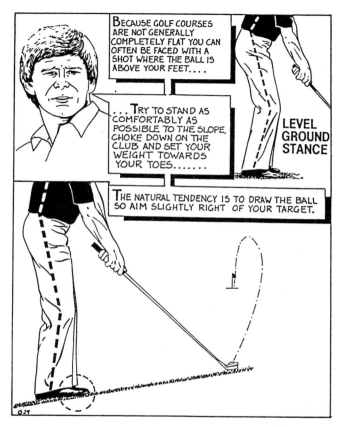

BECAUSE GOLF COURSES ARE NOT GENERALLY COMPLETELY FLAT YOU CAN OFTEN BE FACED WITH A SHOT WHERE THE BALL IS ABOVE YOUR FEET....

...TRY TO STAND AS COMFORTABLY AS POSSIBLE TO THE SLOPE, CHOKE DOWN ON THE CLUB AND SET YOUR WEIGHT TOWARDS YOUR TOES.......

LEVEL GROUND STANCE

THE NATURAL TENDENCY IS TO DRAW THE BALL SO AIM SLIGHTLY RIGHT OF YOUR TARGET.

Ball Above Feet

Ball Below Feet

Divot Marks

Published by EXPRESS BOOKS, 245 Blackfriars Road, London SE1 9UX
Printed by Grosvenor Press (Portsmouth) Ltd; typesetting by Pastiche, London; Reproduction by Graphic Origination, London
and co-ordinated by Roeder Print Services Ltd
Strips by John Huggan. Drawings by Ken Lewis. ©1990 Nick Faldo International